The Old Man and the Tree

A Different Approach to Deer Hunting

Barry Wensel

Copyright © 2023 Barry Wensel

barrywensel@hotmail.com

All rights reserved. No part of this book may be reproduced or transmitted in any form or any means without written permission from the author, except for the inclusion of brief quotations in a review.

This book is a work of non-fiction. Unless otherwise noted, the author and publisher make no explicit guarantee as to the accuracy of the information contained.

ISBN: 9798859437092

DEDICATION

To LeRoy E. Wensel

Mom called him "Lee"; the guys called him "Roy"; my brother and I called him "Dad"

He's the guy who planted the seed for my love of whitetails and whitetail hunting.

He was the guy who patiently showed us the way, who taught my brother and I independence in the timber, then unselfishly stepped aside to encourage our freedom.

Thank you so much Dad. I miss you!

FOREWORD

Growing up in a small town in southcentral Minnesota during the 1990's, I was starved for bowhunting information. I eagerly awaited bowhunting magazines hitting the mailbox, as well as scouring the shelves of the local video rental store for hunting movies. On a cold winter's afternoon, my dad having picked my brother and me up from school, we were each allowed to pick out a movie for the weekend. On the cover of a VHS box was a photo of a pair of bowhunters dragging a buck through a beautiful autumn forest. "Bowhunting October Whitetails" went home with me that day, and I was glued to the movie. Not only were the hunters bagging nice bucks, they were having fun doing it. Especially a short guy with a graying beard and a hat on sideways.

Barry Wensel has, quite literally, been there and done that. In an age of Instagram "professional" hunters beating their chests and killing animals simply for content and clout, Barry is a true woodsman. He hunts for the joy of hunting, has a passion for understanding mature whitetails, and has forgotten more about hunting than most hunters will ever know.

Being asked to help Barry compile his stories and thoughts into books was akin to Michael Jordan tapping a sixth grade hoopster on the shoulder for a game of one-on-one. As an outdoor writer myself, I was excited to help get his words into book form. Sitting in my kitchen, listening to Barry talk about hunting, his twin brother Gene and his friends (including the late, great Paul Schafer), I realized that we are at the end of an era.

Quite simply, he has experiences in the field that will never be duplicated. His decision to write this book is a stroke of luck for all of us hunters. So pull up a chair, sit back, and enjoy the stories and wisdom of the man in the "crooked hat."

Jeffrey Miller, at Cottonwood Bend Farm on the banks of the Sheyenne River, North Dakota.

Author of **Forever Towards the Sunrise: A Lifetime Lived in the Outdoors** and **Klasberg, North Dakota: Collected Stories from the Middle of Nowhere**

ACKNOWLEDGEMENTS

Although my name is listed as the author of this writing, I absolutely could not have done it without the help of various people within my circle of family and friends.

I am most indebted to my immediate family who allowed me to pursue this way of life. Without their generosity very few of these stories and theories would have unfolded. They all understood my need to be free and unselfishly stood in the background with loving attitudes when I often times should have been home.

My two wonderful sons, Jason and Brad, as well as my beautiful daughter, Laurel, have all sacrificed pieces of their lives because of my insatiable hunting habits. I especially must thank my wonderful wife of 56 years, Susan, who so graciously and unselfishly accepted me for what I am. And enabled me to live our lives in areas that allowed me the freedom to pursue my dreams. She truly is the absolute nicest person I've ever met in my life.

A special thank you must go to my brother, Gene. He is not just my only brother but my identical twin, lifelong favorite hunting partner and one of the best whitetail hunters I know. We were often thought of as a "tag-team", no pun intended. Although twins, we are individuals possessing similar, yet different opinions and personalities. The adage "two heads are better than one" has often held true in that it afforded us different ways of challenging and overcoming obstacles, both in the woods and in life.

I have purposely tried not to mention lifelong hunting partners, friends and landowners in order to maintain and respect their privacy. The truth is, if it were not for their generosity and friendships my life would have been very different. They know who they are. And I cannot thank them enough for all these years.

I also must offer a very special thank you to my North Dakota friend, Jeffrey Miller, who so unselfishly offered his expertise in putting these writings together. You, the readers, might have guessed I am better in the woods than I am behind a computer. If it wasn't for Jeffrey, I seriously doubt I would have ever finished this endeavor.

And most of all, I must especially thank God for blessing me with this great life I've lived. He is the one who gathered all these "puzzle pieces" together in order to create the stories and any of my learning experiences to share. We all must be constantly grateful of His infinite wisdom.

Remember that wonderful quote from author Robert Louis Stevenson, " Books are good enough in their way, but they are a mighty bloodless substitute for life."

PREFACE

As the author, I have been a "student of the whitetail" for over sixty years. My whole life has evolved around studying and hunting whitetail deer. I have probably spent as much physical time in the timber as anyone today. When in the woods, I'm a self-proclaimed loner. I'm also a "thinker" who was blessed with some common sense. Yes, a lot of my theories are personal opinions, but they are conclusions formed via trial and error from within real whitetail habitats.

With all the high-technology in today's world, I find it an honor to offer some "not so common knowledge" of whitetail deer and deer hunting, knowing it was learned the old-fashion, natural way via woodsmanship skills and the practical application of those skills with boots on the ground.

It's time to share my philosophies, strategies and hunting techniques that have been so productive for me all these years. I WANT you to succeed in the deer woods. Not just with big antlers and meat on the table but with great memories and fulfilled dreams. I hope to plant the seed of adventure, to spark a burning desire within your core. I also ask you to share any new hunting knowledge with our upcoming generations, so they too will have the opportunities to breathe fresh air, to live life clean, pure and natural as God meant for us.

Thank you!

Barry Wensel

INTRODUCTION

I've been a passionate whitetail deer hunter my whole life. For those who don't know me, I tend to be a loner. To clarify, I love sharing a hunt with friends or family, but when we step into the timber, if my hunting partner goes left, I'll usually go right. It's not that I'm really anti-social as much as it's just that I prefer to go at my own pace. And my pace has been slowing in recent times.

Over the years I've honestly tried hunting with others. It came down to the fact that if I made a mistake, I would learn from it and accept it. But if someone else made a mistake that cost me, I'd have a really hard time accepting it. I understand that's probably some shrink material, but that's just the way it is. Consequently, I tend to hunt and scout on my own or with a very few select individuals.

My identical twin brother, Gene, is an example, yet I don't know if it's a fair example or not. Because we were born eight minutes apart and are very much identical in most physical attributes, there's probably no one I can relate those similarities to as much as my own blood-brother Gene. Over the years there have been times when it was almost unbelievable how precisely similar our thoughts were. It was almost like I could read his mind and I knew what/how he was thinking. I don't mean mental telepathy or mind-speaking per say, but just that I "felt" what he was thinking, and I was very often later proven correct. This obviously made us excellent hunting partners, as well as "two heads are better than one."

On the other side of the coin, we are unique individuals, sometimes with different opinions and beliefs which might be similar but are definitely different.

Over the years because of my age and my nature, I've probably spent as much time in the woods as any man alive. Because of the fact I lived and hunted trophy whitetail areas in Montana, Iowa and other prime states for fifty-plus years, coupled with being self-employed, in generally good health and of a tenacious nature up until just a few years ago made me "unique". Until just recently when extremely managed properties became so common, I probably saw as many, or more, true, wild, free-ranging, huntable Boone and Crockett class whitetail bucks as any one person. No brag… just fact.

Being blessed with a great family who often gave me more freedom than I deserved, I was able to hunt whitetails all over these United States. I had the opportunity to hunt and study these great animals as various sub-species, as well as in diverse terrains and habitats all the way from the Deep South to the Rocky Mountain West, the Canadian front, Central Plains, the mid-west farmlands and New England.

Residing in northwest Montana for almost thirty years I spent a tremendous amount of time hunting on public lands via our U.S. Forest Service, Montana Fish and Game Lands, Bureau of Land Management; National Forest properties, as well as vast, private timber companies who allowed public hunting. Some people looked at this as a negative having to hunt public lands. I think it taught me to adapt accordingly. Often, having to hunt in areas of low deer densities forced me to really buckle down and think in order to succeed. On the other hand, hunting in areas of extremely high deer densities often gave me the opportunity to see things every year that others not as fortunate had never seen in a lifetime of hunting elsewhere.

When living in Montana, studying and hunting whitetails took up probably 90% of my efforts. But I probably should also mention I often hunted other states annually as a non-resident. I remember one fall I hunted whitetails in eight different states. But still, as a resident of Montana I also had the opportunities to hunt a total of ten different big game SPECIES if I drew the proper paperwork. This offered me a lot of additional adventures and experiences in my life.

What you are about to read are my writings accumulated over many decades in hot pursuit of various big game species. Please don't hold me to the exact/specific dates, times, distances, etc. I've really tried to keep it all accurate to the best of my memory and knowledge, but a lot of years have transpired, so please forgive me. I don't consider myself a good writer, but I try to honestly relay the truth as it unfolded to the best of my senile memory.

Also, please forgive the fact some of these chapters were penned many decades ago. I've added to or deleted some from the original content in order to update my present theories. Therefore, some parts might sound or read somewhat familiar. I use the analogy of watching a good, old movie. We all have our classics we've seen several times before but still enjoy watching them again. I recently received a note from a man saying he had just finished reading my book, "Once Upon a Tine" for the third time. It suddenly struck me it wouldn't be so bad to republish some of my old pieces after all, especially if I updated/changed my beliefs. Also, like old movies, we sometimes need to watch them a couple times to pick up some of what we missed the first time around.

You'll hopefully get a sprinkling of variety in the contents coming up. A couple are on species other than whitetails; as stated, some are my old opinions that I might have changed since they were first published; and some are brand-new, never-before-seen chapters that are hopefully both entertaining and educational.

I WANT to share my adventures, strategies and theories with the younger hunters before I take this stuff to the grave with me. I hope to plant the seed of adventure with burning desire in our youth, so they too will have the opportunity to live life clean and pure as God meant it to be.

Thank you and God bless you all.

Barry Wensel

The Old Man and the Tree
TABLE OF CONTENTS

Dedication	*iii*
Foreword	*v*
Acknowledgements	*vii*
Preface	*iv*
Introduction	*x*

Chapter		**Page**
I.	*Point Man*	2
II.	*Waiting for the Man*	18
III.	*Where Do You Start?*	26
IV.	*Ground Level*	34
V.	*Front Row Seat*	44
VI.	*From an Owl to a Cat*	56
VII.	*Now Eye Get It*	76
VIII.	*Tidbits*	84
IX.	*Observations*	94
X.	*Location… Location…*	104
XI.	*Breaking Taboo*	114
XII.	*The Ups and Downs*	124
XIII.	*Ahh… Chew…*	132

XIV.	Pondering	140
XV.	Benign	146
XVI.	Picking Ripe Fruit	156
XVII.	Closing the Deal	170
XVIII.	Dead End	182
XIX.	Thoughts on Scrapes	192
XX.	Not So Obvious Details	202
XXI.	Bear Essentials	216
XXII.	Proper Virtues	230
XXIII.	Happy Anniversary	242
XXIV.	Stand Choices	250
XXV.	Still Hunting	258
XXVI.	Coming Full Boar	270
XXVII.	The Midas Touch	282
XXVIII.	Southern Exposure	288
XXIX.	The Hundred-Year-Old Man	298

CHAPTER I
POINT MAN

All three of my children participated in sports. As parents, sometimes our lives were spread pretty thin. Often, we found myself going to one game and my wife to another to show our support.

I remember one particular baseball game in the mid-1980s when our youngest son, Brad, was pitching. Brad was a gifted athlete who consistently pulled off incidents I just shook my head in disbelief at.

I'm thinking he was maybe eight or nine years old. I personally watched him pull off three totally unassisted triple plays in one baseball game. As an example, like I said, he was pitching. There was a runner on first and second base. The batter hit a line drive and Brad caught it. That guy is out. Brad instantly, without apparent thinking, runs to the guy who was on first, going to second and tags him out. Then, since he had his running momentum already in gear and was naturally fast anyway, he continued on and easily tagged the guy who was on second base. We win... the umps look at each other and shrug their shoulders... game over... done deal.

On the ride home I told him how proud I was of him, etc. but then I asked him just how he did what he did? I said, "it was almost like you knew what was going to happen before it actually happened." I said, "seriously, how did you know that was going to happen?" His answer kind of floored me. He said (sort of), "whenever I'm in any situation like that, I always think about what I need to do in case each possible scenario actually happens." In other words, he prepares his mind to counter whatever MIGHT happen so he already knows how to adjust accordingly to his benefit, instinctively without having to think about it.

I said, "Who taught you that?" He said he didn't know. I'd like to take credit but I know I didn't. Remember, he's about 9 years old. Here's a nine-year-old kid teaching me, his adult father, how to think ahead on scenarios that life might throw at you. It must be he takes after his mother!

I'm not too proud to admit I learned from a nine-year-old. It's a life lesson that we all need to consider. That lesson helped me get another Iowa corn-fed giant buck with my recurve at under 15 yards a few years ago. Bear with me.

Please follow along with this tale that spans several seasons as it gives us a good opportunity to learn.

Mid-November 2015 I was on my way into an afternoon/evening short ladder stand in a tiny juniper not six inches in diameter at my back. Granted, it wasn't a great tree but it was in the right spot guarding a funnel/pinch-point just above a header (the head of an eroded/dry seepage) in a great area.

Because the platform was only maybe seven feet above ground level and the softwood was rather thin to begin with, I wore my Ghillie suit as I often do in these circumstances. It's worked well for me over the years.

Stopping fifty yards short of the ladder stand, I leaned my recurve against a tree and put on my Ghillie. I was just finishing adjusting my armguard when I glanced up and here he comes.

He was a beautiful, prime 5.5-year-old Iowa stud. He had those long, curved tines that measure longer than they actually appear. I was struck by his distinct white throat patch. He was what I'd call handsome. I wanted him!

Walking through the header he was about halfway to my unoccupied ladder stand when he saw me kneeling. The instant I had first seen him I had dropped down to one knee and nocked an arrow. You have to realize I am in full camo with the Ghillie suit, Ghillie hat and facemask, kneeling low profile on red alert. He never saw me move but he questioned the "clump." We had the big stare-down for what seemed like forever. Squinting my eyes to minimize eye-contact he accepted me. Whew!

Turning broadside he continued on his way cruising for a hot chick. All I had to do was pull back and shoot him. But as he slowly picked his way through the saplings I realized although he appeared in the open, there were a lot of two-inch second-growth saplings between us. Being honest with myself I gave it a 50/50 chance of getting an arrow into his ribs at about 20 yards. I don't like 50/50 odds on big bucks. So, I hesitated and elected to let him walk away in hopes he'd meet a girlfriend a little farther up on the ridge. If he did, and that was quite likely, there would be an excellent chance she'd bring him back through the pinch where I'd be in my stand by then.

To add salt to my wounds, just ten yards from the base of my ladder stand he demolished a poor tree, then gave me a glance over his shoulder for approval, then walked away. It was like he was insulting me. Game on buddy!

Is that a big antler laying there?

Fast forward to March 2016. I was holding one of my Whitetail Bootcamp sessions. Walking through a dry creek bed with fifteen guys in tow, something caught my eye. At least a hundred yards up the dry creek on the bank I stopped and pointed saying, "Is that a big antler laying up there?" One of the young guys with long legs ran up, bringing it back saying, "you gotta be kidding me!" Of course, I got accused of planting the shed, but I swear to God I didn't. The sunlight just hit it right. At any rate, it was the same buck's left shed and added another piece to my pursuit.

Late October 2016 I was in a morning stand a half mile away from the first encounter. Looking up at "pink light" here he comes. He was strikingly beautiful. I noticed he grew some small stickers on his new rack but it was definitely him. He was now 6.5 years old and in his prime. He might or might not measure Boone and Crockett but it didn't matter to me.

Twenty-seven yards wasn't close enough in 2016

Now, my big problem! The summer of 2016 I had open heart surgery. On September 1st I couldn't draw a 30 lb. bow.

Gradually increasing my bow poundage by our season opener on October 1st, with effort, I could put three arrows in a three-inch group at eighteen yards. But because of my inability to practice without pain I promised myself not to take any shots over about fifteen yards. Friends said, "but yeah… but he's a monster buck." In my opinion that was all the more reason not to gamble on a questionable shot. That's just the way I am. And

I'm proud to say I killed two big 160-inch bucks in 2016 and both were ten-yard shots.

Back to the story, his line of travel that morning brought him by me at what I figured to be 27 yards. He was standing broadside in the open timber without a clue the boogieman was right there holding a taut string. In the old days when I was in my prime it would have been all over right then. But being honest with myself I didn't get that warm fuzzy feeling I could make the shot. I knew I could probably hit him but I wasn't completely confident on a clean kill-shot exactly where I wanted it. That tiny seed of negativity kept me from shooting. So, as hard as it was, I let him walk away. The fact it was still only October and early in the season also entered my mind. Although I got some trail camera pictures and some short trail camera video clips later didn't help because he was absolutely gorgeous. The hard fact remained I never actually laid eyes on him again for the rest of the 2016 season.

Late October 2017 I was sitting tucked into a big, bushy, thick cedar tree. Because it was a softwood, the needles held on when the first couple frosts always dropped the surrounding fall foliage. The stand was purposely kept low so the thinning upper branches wouldn't skyline and backlight me. The foot platform of the old hang-on Screaming Eagle stand was only six feet in elevation, but I was tucked in and the winds were perfect and consistent. Yes, six feet is really low but it doesn't matter when you are tucked in with great cover around and behind you and good steady advantageous wind directions. I prefer a little wind for consistency. If you have NO wind scent tends to pool around you and drift here and there. And too much velocity has everything moving. The deer don't like that and tend to move into more open terrain. I prefer a nice steady breeze of 6 or 8

MPH.

The front of the stand faced almost due north. I had cleared one shooting hole in front of me at about 12 o'clock and another off my left side at the 9 o'clock position. At about eighteen yards to the NNW is a single, twelve-inch diameter oak tree. Because of its natural position there has always been an active scrape under the tree for at least the last twenty years. Ten yards to the northwest of the scrape is a fence corner. A barbed-wire fence runs east/west then north from that fence corner-post. It creates a structural funnel that pinches deer movement right to the scrape tree. Multiple bucks hammer it annually, including the one on the front cover of this book.

I've had a trail camera on the scrape for years. The results often show what potential is on the menu... plus, wandering bucks often show up as an additional bonus. So, usually in late August or early September (at least a month before our October 1st. opener) I'll go in and detail the stand for the fall. I'll take a hand sickle and/or a weedwhacker and open up the prominent, already established deer trails some more. Sometimes I'll also open up a new trail or two to shift some movement that might be advantageous for where I want them to walk.

To the west of the stand there is a trail that runs north/south at about 12 yards. There is also a second primary trail running east/west about fourteen yards to the north of the stand. As stated above, depending on the annual understory growth, I might alter them a little to my advantage if needed. I don't mean major changes but maybe shift the existing trail ten feet or so towards my stand position. Or another example would be to lay a limb or drop a sapling to cover one "Y" of a forked trail for my advantage. Think ahead and give them time to adapt to your minor changes.

I'll also take my trusty hoe and rake away the grass down to bare dirt, to create a "visual" in order to entice deer to walk the easiest route where I want them to go. I also rake out the location of the previous year's scrape and doctor it up with some of Smokey's pre-orbital glandular scent on the overhanging limbs and maybe a little interdigital scent in the scrape itself, then hang a trail camera, back out and leave it alone for weeks.

Over the years I've had some of my best days afield the last few days of October and the first few of November. It seems most people always prefer mid-November as their favorite time to hunt because of the peak of the rut. Don't get me wrong as mid-November is great but my favorite time is the end of October and early November. My reasoning is based on the buck's demeanor. In late October the bucks are ready but the does are not. That buck anxiety will generate outstanding daytime mature buck movement. Bucks will be cruising slowly, walking around from one doe bedding area to the next, trying to find that first pretty doe that comes into heat. I much prefer the slow, steady gait of a wandering, single, stud buck in late October over the frantic chasing of multiple does that all came into heat near the same time, with a string of running bucks flying by me at full speed in hot pursuit. Granted, that's a sight to behold, but it often leaves us standing with our jaws dropped open, a poor at best rushed shot, or maybe an arrow still on the string with us shaking our heads negatively on what just happened.

Additionally, in my opinion, THE best scrape activity is during a cold front in late October. Mature bucks cruising for that first hot doe, figuratively peeing on every fire hydrant in the neighborhood leads me to favor this time of year over mid-November.

As I've preached for many years, the morning of the first hard frost of the year is ALWAYS one of the best days of hunting the entire season. Plan that day sitting in a great funnel and you'll be glad you bought this book! The does might not be ready but the bucks are and they'll be flaunting it. Calling, grunting, rattling and wheezing also come into play. Plan ahead and take that info to the bank!

Like my young son Brad taught me, think about the possibilities. Prepare for the unknown. Another good analogy is the standard military procedure of sending out a point-man to look for problems so the mass formation of troops won't fall into a trap or ambush.

Yet another great example was during the days of our pioneer frontiersmen, both military and settlers. They would hire an "Indian scout" to test the waters of unknown territories before the troops or wagon trains followed into potential unsafe grounds. Again... plan ahead.

Relate this knowledge back to the stand outlined above how my early preparation came into play. Because of all the pieces of the puzzle this stand, which is nick-named "Screamer", is best hunted on a wind from the northwest. Entrance either morning or evening is from the southeast. Don't hold me to the dates/times but I'm thinking it was October 30, 2017. We had that first cold, hard frost of the year I spoke of earlier that morning. At 8:32 I had a single, mature doe crest the hill fifty yards to the northwest of my perch. She jumped the fence in the corner and trotted right past me at 10 or 12 yards going south right through my left shooting hole. It was very obvious she was being chased. Her tongue was hanging out and she was gasping for air. Something was pushing her hard. There was no question in my mind on what was about to happen.

Now, here comes the important part. I stood on red alert with bow in hand waiting for whoever/whatever was pushing her. Now remember, there are two major trails I am guarding. One is right in front of me at fourteen yards going west/east and the other off my left side at about twelve yards going north/south. I assumed whatever was chasing her would be scent-trailing her and would likely take the same trail she followed. There was probably an 80% to 90% chance of that happening.

BUT... what if he lost her track and took the west/east run right in front of me? Like my young son, I had to prepare myself for that possibility. Think ahead like Brad taught me. I'm right-handed and shoot my bow instinctively. If I knew I was going to be shooting off my left side, playing the odds, shooting at the 9 o'clock position, I'd likely point the toes of my boots straight north (12 o'clock) to shoot off my left side. BUT... what if he didn't take that trail to my left? What if he might lose her trail and take that west/east trail right in front of me? I would have been forced to torque my whole body to the right (clockwise) which is an uncomfortable angle for any right-handed bowhunter, especially one shooting a traditional recurve bow instinctively. So, in order to adjust for that possibility, I pointed the toes of my boots to the right at about 1 or 2 o'clock because it'd be easier to torque my body to the left than twisting, rotating to the right.

Scraping with Intensity

I slipped the lower limb of my recurve into the tiny pocket I have sewn just above the knee of my left pant leg explicitly for situations like this. With the lower limb tip in the little pocket all

The Old Man and the Tree

The end of the trail

you have to do is balance the weight of the bow rather than fatiguing my left arm holding it at red alert for longer periods. I stood there perfectly still... waiting. I was ready.

Unbelievably, it took him a full twenty minutes to arrive. Here he came, cresting the horizon about 75 yards to the northwest trotting right to me. Here was the interesting part that I'd never seen before and I'll remember for the rest of my life. He had his head down like a beagle scent-tracking a cottontail, but his hair was all bristled up; his ears laid back in aggressive posturing and... he was growling. I don't mean any kind of tending grunt, I mean a downright steady, deep growl similar to a dog on the verge of biting you. And I want to impress it wasn't just for a few seconds but was a steady growl from the time he first crested the horizon. It was very obvious he was trying to track this hot doe; he was THE MAN; he had lost her trail somewhat and he was PISSED she wasn't making it easy.

As he approached the scrape tree he came up off his front legs and dove headlong into the overhanging limbs seven or eight feet above ground level. He whipped the branches with such fury he broke one thumb-sized limb off and tossed it over his shoulder. And all this time he was viciously growling. Then he dropped into the scrape and violently gouged three or four destructive swipes with each front hoof, throwing dirt and debris twenty feet to the rear, again growling the whole time. It was very impressive.

Then, here he came onward towards me. He was not really running but walking fast, nose to the ground, ears laid back, still all bristled up and growling. He would for sure be very intimidating to any other bucks he encountered.

Thank you Brad!

I assumed he would continue on the doe track and follow her trail past me on my left. But to my surprise, when he came to where her trail crossed the west/east run straight in front of me he quickly turned, again losing her track and walked right in front of me at probably thirteen yards headed east. The fact is I was totally prepared for that last, split-second move on his part. I swung on him choosing not to audibly stop him in full stride and let the string slip from my fingers. My arrow, tipped with a razor-sharp Woodsman broadhead, took him a few inches behind his heart, angled slightly forward, punched through the far side of his chest, then reburied into the fleshy "bicep" of his front left upper leg.

He tore out of there heading straight south behind me. I heard him crash less than a hundred yards away. I took a deep breath, smiled and thanked God for my life and this unforgettable experience. And I also thanked a nine-year-old kid who taught me to think ahead in life, be it at home, work, on the baseball field or in the timber. Prepare ourselves for possible upcoming circumstances.

For those who are interested in the stats, the buck was later proven to be the 7.5-year-old that I had previously passed up, for one reason or another the two previous seasons. He was a basic 6x6 frame, plus forked brow tines and good mass with heavy 6 5/8-inch circumference bases between the burr and brows. He green measured a little over 174 inches. Thank you Brad!

"Your greatest weapon is your mind"

CHAPTER II
WAITING FOR THE MAN

I've always said we have deer hunters, buck hunters and trophy buck hunters. When we have a big, fully mature stud whitetail buck with a giant set of antlers step out into the field alongside a big, fat, plump, juicy doe... 999 out of 1,000 hunters will take the big buck even though the doe will likely make better table fare. That's just human nature and the way it is.

Yes, they somewhat look alike but a big, fully mature buck is almost a different critter. They tend to be so different than the rest of the herd you almost have to pursue them as a separate specie. Throughout my writings you will continually hear me use the phrase "fully mature buck." This is important to note in the respect I don't consider a buck "fully" mature until he's 5.5 years old.

I get a personal kick out of these outdoor TV show guys. They'll be doing a half-hour show on bowhunting whitetails. About twenty-five minutes into the show, they'll make the announcement it's the last day of their hunt, so they'll be breaking out the (also legal) gun. I guess that's okay, but more than half the time they end up shooting an immature buck and try to justify their actions by saying it's a "mature 3.5-year-old buck." When in reality, a 3.5 or even a 4.5-year-old buck is not mature in my estimation. They are the teenagers of the deer world. They're somewhere between puberty and youthful juveniles in my opinion, but certainly not a "man."

Again, I don't consider a whitetail buck "a man" until he's at least 5.5 years. I've had guys argue a 4.5-year-old buck from a heavily hunted region is smarter than a 4.5-year-old buck from a remote wilderness area. That could hold some merit since a deer develops his intelligence partially through genetics and partially from memories of past experiences. They absolutely remember. And a buck from a heavily hunted area will likely have more opportunities for up close and personal learning experiences than a truly wilderness buck. That, in my opinion, is more psychological. Physiologically or anatomically, two 4.5-year-old bucks are the same no matter what region they come from.

Once they reach that 5.5-year-old bracket they become "different." Their personalities change. Inherited, genetic traits surface and each becomes a specific/ unique individual. And they must be hunted differently than the majority of the herd. It is these fully mature, older and unique individuals that test our hunting skills to the maximum. For those of us that cherish the hunt itself, we have turned the page into a new chapter of deer hunting.

I like to refer to them as "slow walkers." When they finally reach full maturity every single move they make is under calculated scrutiny. All their decisions are usually totally dependent on messages received from their eyes, ears, noses and memories.

I often use analogies in order to understand my thought processes more easily. Compare domesticated dogs as an example with deer. Each dog has a single, unique, distinct personality. That's probably why they are "man's best friend." I personally believe a specific deer's personality is developed both via inherited genetic traits as well as personal life experiences. Within any regional deer herd or family group you will have roamers and home-bodies; loners and groupies; passive and aggressive (lovers and fighters) which include bullies as well as shy animals. Then, throw in personality changes that take place only at certain times of the year, in example, the rut. Comparatively, one dog will run up to you wagging his tail and licking you, whereas another may challenge you or even bite you.

These truths also dictate different ways we best hunt each "personality." As stated previously, they tend to be so different than the rest of the herd they need to be hunted almost like a different species. Again, big, mature bucks are different.

An excellent example I will lay out here will let people more easily understand their normal, everyday lives. These are the fine pieces of the puzzle that will change the way you hunt and will offer so much more enjoyment in your pursuit.

Say we have a hardwood ridge running east/west with a food source as a field at the bottom of the ridge to the north (i.e., an alfalfa field.) As the reader I want you to understand these facts. Feel free to sketch them out on a piece of scrap paper if it will help you to understand the concept.

It's simple science. Hot air rises and cold air sinks because it's heavier. Because whitetails tend to be more nocturnal critters, they instinctively take advantage of these facts. We'll get into the specific reasoning a little later but right now I want to plant the seed of how big bucks are different than the rest of the herd.

Remember, our nights are their days and our days are their nights. During the warmth of the day the air temps will rise resulting in up-drifting thermals. The family group, consisting of mature does, yearlings, fawns and immature bucks will be near the top of the ridge on the leeward side (we'll get to this later).

Scrutinize the beds. When I was young, I'd see where a half dozen deer were bedded. I'd hardly break stride and move on. Since I've gotten a lot older my age has made me slow down. Frankly, this is a good thing in that it gives us more time to think. Think about what you are seeing. This is a VERY important habit to get into. It will change you as a hunter forever.

Over the years I've been asked what single attribute all really successful whitetail hunters seem to have. There are multiple answers. Some say they have to have good game eyes; others will say they have to be self-employed, retired or even independently wealthy (WRONG!) in order to afford the time it takes to learn. The one factor I have noticed ALL exceptional whitetailers to possess is they are all THINKERS.

Slow down and think about what you are seeing. There's almost always a reason why they are doing what they're doing. And when you come up with your own theory, share it with others. Plant the seed to those who are interested and discuss different opinions on what you're seeing. They might come up with a slightly different opinion or view that can be added to your opinion. Looking at something from just a slightly different angle can sometimes completely change the concept. This is how we learn. If a theory proves itself correct enough times it eventually becomes fact.

As I stated above, think about what you are seeing. Age tends to slow us down. This is a good thing. It makes us THINK. But realize you don't have to get old before you start slowing down to think for knowledge and wisdom. Remember, there's a fine line between wisdom and senility... but don't quote me on that.

When I was a young hunter, I freely admit I didn't take the time to study what I was looking at. I was always in a rush to learn everything as soon as I could. That is hopefully one of my gifts to you, the readers. I only wish I knew as a young man what I know now. Hopefully some of this woodsmanship knowledge will start questioning what you are seeing and that in turn will place your knowledge way ahead of the process I went through. Not slowing down was a huge error on my part. Resist the tendency to move on too quickly.

This is where I like to use the analogy of looking at an x-ray. If someone slaps an x-ray up on the screen, any layman can look at it and point out the various anatomical parts. There's the skull; there's the spine; there's the pelvis, etc. But when a doctor/radiologist looks at that same x-ray he's looking for fine details such as hairline fractures, any degenerations or calcium infiltration, etc. He's looking for DETAILS. And that is exactly what we must do in our learning curve while in the timber. Educate yourself on what you're seeing.

Back to the deer beds. If you scrutinize that cluster of deer beds, you'll notice some details. The bed itself is shaped like a lima bean or kidney bean. Wet leaves or snow make it obvious. In fact, when deer usually bed down in the mornings the leaves on the ground are usually cool and moist from the dew. Their body heat tends to dry out those damp leaves resulting in a flat "ironed" bed if they bedded for any length of time. Wet leaves or snow make it obvious. You can tell which way they were facing. As an example, say you are looking at a half dozen beds from a family group bedded yesterday in a previous two-inch snowfall. Notice the majority of the beds were laying with the wind at their backs. But also notice they are slightly bedded at different angles so they have eyes covering all angles of intrusion their noses don't pick up.

This is fairly common knowledge but I'll mention it here since everyone may not be familiar with it. You can look at a deer bed in the snow and often tell if the bed was from a buck or doe. When a relaxed deer arises from its bed, the first thing they frequently do is void their bladder, generally even before they step out of the bed. Anatomically, a doe is built differently than a buck. Look for the yellow urine spot in the snow. If it was a doe bed the yellow spot would be right on the periphery of the bed. It's similar to the outer dripline of a tree or an umbrella. Whereas when a buck steps up from his bed the yellow urine spot will be more centered like a bullseye because of his physical anatomy. Either way, don't eat the yellow snow boys and girls! One other thing to consider, bucks tend to "dribble" more while they are actually bedded, therefore you may find more melting in the center buck's urine spot.

I probably should also mention that both sexes often do the "cat stretch" and immediately defecate as soon as they stand up from the bed. So, if you find pellets right in the bed it is usually of no great value if it is a buck or doe in my opinion.

The main point in these last few paragraphs is the fact you'll almost never find the big, mature bucks bedded with the family group. He might or might not be close, but he'll normally separate himself from the main group. And he'll often use his separate bedding spot to take advantage of the positioning of the main herd for his own security. He'll use the rest of them to his advantage... like the King's throne overlooking his peasants.

Once in a while he may have a good up and coming 3.5 or 4.5-year-old buck bedded near himself. I'm not convinced if he's using the younger buck to his advantage or if the younger buck is using him as a learning tool. But normally the big boys are loners.

Now, back to the basics no one seems to understand. I'll likely include this info elsewhere because it's important, so bear with me. They lay in their beds most of the day facing downhill to the north in this scenario. In the afternoon, the herd consisting of mature does, immature adolescent bucks; does, yearlings and fawns will rise from their beds, stretch and slowly start to descend the mountain towards the food source, using the up-drifting thermal currents to their advantage for security. I also think they are often using that buck still laying in his bed as security to cover the back door for themselves as well.

But the point is that big, fully mature trophy buck is an entirely different critter compared to the rest of the herd. The man stays in his bed until the sun goes down and the air temps start to cool. When that happens, the thermal drift starts to change. Cool air is heavier than warm air so the cooling air temps reverse the direction the warm thermals have been drifting all day and slowly start to descend the mountain. THEN is when the big trophy buck stands up from his bed and starts down the mountain.

People ask why a big buck will do that knowing the wind (thermal air currents) are now at his back and he's now walking blindly not able to smell any danger in front of himself. The answer is rather brilliant in that now he can smell anything behind him (uphill and upwind) but at the same time he has the entire rest of the deer herd (the original pre-mentioned family group) already out in the field at the food source below (north) acting like decoys drawing attention away from himself. If we should get boogered by one button-buck fawn you won't even know the man was around. He has used the rest of the herd to his advantage to maintain his personal security. That's just the way it is.

Think about it. That's the very reason he's usually the very last one to step out into the field just before dark. And the exact opposite (reverse) is true the next morning. The biggest trophy buck is usually the first one to leave the field in the morning, often when it's still dark and even before pink light. He heads up the mountain with the descending, cool thermal currents in his face and the rest of the herd to his rear safely covering the back door. Think about what you are seeing.

"There's a difference between being aware of the wind direction and actually using it to your advantage"

CHAPTER III
WHERE DO YOU START?

One of the most common questions I'm asked about hunting a new property is "where do you start?" For about twenty years when I was a younger man, I did private land consulting work. Landowners would hire me to walk their properties to ribbon off the potentially better treestand sites.

I walked dozens of properties all the way from New England to Alberta, Canada. I averaged about 200 acres per day of huntable property. In example, if one landowner had 400 acres of property that was 50% cultivated fields, it wouldn't take as long as his neighbor who also had 400 acres but it was all timber. Using that example of 400 acres of solid timber, I'd walk it for about two days alone and ribbon off trees, then the third day I'd walk it with the landowner and explain my findings and/or suggestions. I preferred walking it alone at first so I could think about what I was seeing, rather than having to converse and/or hear "war stories" of previous hunts and sightings. This worked out well in the respect it gave the property owner another opinion to consider, or at least to hopefully validate his own thinking.

There's a huge difference walking a property for someone else, especially when you're on the timeclock, versus walking one for yourself when there are no time restrictions. When you have all the time in the world, I prefer leaving no stone unturned. Note, I've changed my opinion on this in my older age. It used to be I preached having a preference to scout a property once for six hours, rather than three times for two hours each time. My thinking was that if I scouted it for six hours straight, I'd only disturb the area one time (for six hours).

Since I've gotten old, I found I've cut back because of my physical inabilities to scout for six hours straight (even though I slowed the pace.) Nowadays, I prefer to scout three different times for a couple hours each rather than once for six hours. Not only do the physical efforts not kill me anymore, but I'm also allowed to see patterns I wasn't able to see in one six-hour session. I.E. I can compare wind directions for three separate days rather than only one.

To get started in any new, unfamiliar property I first like a SHORT visit with the landowner or property manager. I want to verify his boundaries so I know I'm not trespassing. I don't really want him going with me, but I do appreciate any basics such as: "that back field extends around the corner of that visible timber in an "L" shape. There are beans in it this year, but it'll be corn next year", etc. Then... just turn me loose.

The very first thing I do is to look for any drainages on the property. I don't care if they have water in them or not, as long as I can access both sides. I'll first walk the entire length of any creek and note the major creek crossings. Then, after locating those, I'll take each crossing uphill on each side of the creek. You'll usually find shelves that parallel each side of the main drainage. You'll notice the higher up the side of the ridge you go the narrower the drainage/seepage becomes. These seepages/tributaries are normally dry, other than a recent rainfall or melt-off. Make sure you follow each side seepage all the way up the hillside. Very often at, or near, the top you'll find what I refer to as a "header." A header is the highest point near where those sidehill tributaries start. Usually just a few feet to a

Where Do You Start?

Creek bottom deer sign

couple yards above the header will be an easy/flat crossing where deer will be able to parallel the main creek bottom and not have to cross the side drainage below the header. These headers, near a flat shelf that parallel the main drainage, are often major pinch-points of travel along the ridge lines. These are often excellent potential ambush spots that need to be considered.

Also, remember the higher you get on the parallel ridges the more consistent the winds will be compared to the bottoms. Access to these header-stands is often pretty good. Depending on the area and time of day, time of year, etc. if you come in below, you can use the washout itself in the creek bottom to slip in out of sight.

Another positive people often don't think about is the fact entrance/exit is much quieter in the creek bottom itself. Often, fallen foliage will litter the shelves in the timber making access along the ridge poor at best. But the dry leaves that have fallen in the creek drainage have often been washed aside by any recent rains, exposing clear sand, clay or exposed rocks instead of cornflakes. Not to mention your silhouette is right down in the creek bottom itself out of sight rather than being skylighted like you might be up on the hill.

Depending on how high up the ridge your stand is, and how wide the valley below is, you can sometimes get into your header-stands from above with minimal disturbance. This, by the way, is one of the most critical points no matter where you hunt. ALWAYS try to hunt undisturbed deer. Hunting undisturbed animals will allow them to act the way they are supposed to be acting. It will allow you some dependable consistencies instead of them being in a survival mode all the time.

Even flat terrain will have some structure for water drainage. Water drainage means more moisture. And more moisture usually means more vegetation along the drainages. More vegetation means more density and more density means more security for all the wildlife. These strips of thicker growth dictate secure travel corridors for all the local critters. Even if these minor tributaries are dry, the resulting growth will have restricted the parallel farming practices from any adjoining cultivated crops. Even a minor tributary or possible hedgerow will offer security cover; shade; browse; bedding; occasional water; windbreaks, etc. Also notice if the predominant wind direction runs perpendicular to the tributary (at right angles) most of the game movement will be on the downwind side. For example, if the tributary runs north/south and the predominate winds come from the west, northwest or southwest, there will be more natural game movement on the east side of that tributary.

Often it depends on the thickness or width of the growth paralleling the tributary, but it again, makes perfect sense. They will smell what they can't see and see what they can't smell.

While I think of it, I'll also mention this. Say you have a square, open field with one single tree growing in the middle of that field. Say, the farmer left that single big oak in the middle of that field as a shade tree if he ever had cattle in there. Because he couldn't plant crops right next to that tree, weeds created a little "island" around it. Depending on the density and size of that island, deer might even occasionally bed under it, or feed on the dropping acorns in the fall. The same with other predators and prey. Critters could come all around it and still have some cover and shade.

To use this example even a little farther, say the top of the square field is north and a big old buck wants to walk across that big open field south to north. The prevailing winds come from the west in this scenario. A couple points we must consider. First off, a buck will use that single tree to take the

Excellent deer sign in a creek bed

attention off himself. He'll use that single tree as "cover" in order to draw attention away from himself in the wide open. If that single tree was not there and the field was within eyesight of a county road on the west side, he would stop walking when a vehicle drove by, minimizing movement so as not to draw attention to himself. But, with that single tree there, he will 99 times out of 100 pass by on the downwind (east) side of that tree in order to scent check it, rather than passing it blindly. That's just the way it is and we must adapt accordingly.

In this scenario a hunter might consider setting up in a single tree himself. That might work for a gun hunter but if you are bowhunting, knowing the buck will likely be passing downwind of you, you'd be much better off to follow the approximate line of travel and set up on the downwind side (east side) of the linear south to north movement where he enters the timber on the north side of the field.

Back to scouting the main timbered area and first checking out the situation on what you are dealing with. I again must stress we need to scrutinize the details. Don't just follow the main trails. Walk every minor trail you see. Remember, if there is a huge track there, he was there for a reason.

I'll confess here I used to be pretty sneaky obtaining my info towards pieces of the puzzle. If someone I knew, or I even didn't know, killed a big buck I would try to talk him into showing me the exact spot where it all went down. I'd use the line, "the buck's already dead, you got him. I just want to picture it in my dreams how you tricked him." Build on his ego.

You need to consider the fact the hunter is still on cloud nine, ready and often willing to brag on his success, especially when I say, "the deer's dead... you got him buddy!"

This works especially well if the guy is not a hardcore hunter. The fact is he might have stumbled into the buck and likely will never even hunt the area again for the rest of his life. What he shares with me may be totally useless to him and priceless to me. Yes... I'm sometimes sneaky. You still like me don't you?

Take in all the pieces of the puzzle. Often guys disregard valuable pieces of info. A good example is old sign. They'll look at a giant old rub and say to themselves, "he's already dead." What he often fails to realize is an up and coming 4.5- year- old subordinate buck might decide to use that area in the same way as his grand- daddy did next year. Even old sign designates travel patterns. It might not be relevant now, yet it might be later.

The same goes with old scrapes. Guys will often look at an old, dried-up scrape and mentally turn the page because it was made in November and it is now April. It DOES matter. Study that old sign. I'm not going to say "sign is forever" but I'm going to say you can learn a lot from a big breeding scrape if you study them. Try to figure out a pattern. They are there for a reason. I can walk you into areas I haven't stepped foot in for thirty years and point out spots we haven't even been up to yet. I can tell you all about that scrape because it's been there every year for thirty years, likely because of the terrain. When a guy starts to think like a big old buck and can correctly predict his movements before the buck actually makes the move, that's when you can smile, knowing you are getting there.

"Scouting leads to understanding; understanding leads to confidence; confidence leads to patience; and patience leads to success"

Chapter IV
GROUND LEVEL

I've always been a big believer in order to consistently kill big, fully mature whitetail bucks your best bet is to be in an elevated tree stand letting them come to you. But that's not the only way.

I love to vary my hunting techniques simply for variety. Still-hunting, spot and stalk, tracking or small pushes/nudges add spice to the hunts. All the above are done at ground level. But in all honesty, in order to consistently (with emphasis on consistently) get the really big bucks you normally must remain motionless with an advantageous wind and let them come to you. Ground level pretty much leaves us with ground blinds, either natural or artificial. By artificial I'm referring to pop-up blinds. I'm going to be right up front and confess here I've never killed a whitetail from a pop-up blind. Not that I couldn't have since I presently own three good quality pop-ups. I've killed warthogs, baboons and my big bull sable in Zimbabwe from pop-up blinds, but never a whitetail because of circumstances. Hunting success from pop-up blinds varies greatly with the species you're hunting. In other words, hunting whitetails versus turkeys will usually be vastly different. Generally speaking, pop-ups for whitetails must be well hidden and brushed in considerably in order to achieve success. The only variable will be if you erect a portable blind and give it a long time for local deer to accept as an inanimate object of no threat. Then, you also need to consider extremely secure tie-downs to accommodate higher winds over the extended time of acceptance.

I personally feel natural blinds are far superior for a surprise ambush, again with emphasis on the word "surprise". Especially when used with a good quality Ghillie suit. I ordered my ghillie and it's not a paid endorsement but it's served me well for decades. (**www.ranchosafari.com**) I had mine custom made in the lighter weight material since they sometimes tend to be hot in warmer temperatures. I also chose a combination of the Mossy Oak Shadow Grass pattern as the base with jute/burlap. I personally feel a lot of the standard ghillie camo colors appear to be too dark, likely because of military usage after dark. Whereas the slightly lighter Mossy Oak patterns blend perfectly in the hardwoods and weeds of our Midwest timber and prairies. I personally only ordered the ¾ length because I found that was all that was necessary when shooting from a seated position or occasionally standing in brush.

One factor you might need to be aware of is the fact some companies have their brands listed differently by size. i.e., all ghillies from Ranchosafari are approximately the same size/cut in the body (if ordering you might want to verify this). But when ordering, your specific sizing is adjusted according to your body height. In other words, since I normally wear a size 2XL but I'm "vertically challenged", I ordered mine in size Small. It's the only size Small I can get into since high school days. I want to stress how important a good ghillie suit is to have when needed. I wear mine a lot more than people realize. It's an option not only when still-hunting but also when hunting from cedars, junipers or any pines. I also find myself using it a lot in the late seasons after the foliage has cleared.

Spandoflage facemask

Make sure you order the ghillie hat. It's my opinion the ghillie hat is absolutely the most important part of the entire outfit. In fact, I find it hard to believe a good ghillie hat with lots of burlap strips and jute hanging off the sides isn't the most popular hunting hat out there. It's more functional in the field than any hunting lid I know of. The only alteration I make is to trim a few of the shaggy strips in the front so as not to get them tangled in my bowstring. I always wear a thin Spandoflage stretchy facemask anyway. Because the hat is so shaggy, it eliminates the appearance of a human head sitting atop the shoulders of a predator, which is an extremely important factor.

I've tried still-hunting in my ghillie and although it's very effective, it might tend to hang-up and catch on to all briars, twigs, understory and cling-ons. And like my buddy, Mike Prescott says, "If you ain't in the cling-ons... you ain't in the bucks." But there are areas with tight overhead canopies and minimal understory, open sage brush, dry creek beds, etc. where ghillies work great for still-hunting.

Most of the time I've pretty much settled on carrying my suit rolled up until I get to, or close to, my ambush site. A rolled up ghillie, with hat included, is only about sixteen inches long and maybe eight inches in diameter. Most have a carrying strap included. For closer ambush sites I tend just to throw the ghillie strap over my shoulder and carry any stool in by hand. If you are going in deeper you can bungee the suit and the stool on to a simple pack frame to keep your hands free.

As previously stated, I prefer to keep my profile low to the ground/cover. I therefore usually sit on a good, quiet stool. Being able to sit quietly will keep your movements minimal, which is vitally important when dealing with game at eye level and ultra-close ranges. Whenever possible, I prefer to get into a shallow pit, log jam, wash-out or an uprooted tree well.

Picking the right spot for a ground blind is just as important as picking the right tree for a treestand. And maybe it's more important because of scent and closeness. You usually have no room for error. Setting up with the wind to your advantage is a no brainer. But with minimal to no winds, one must be aware that scent will pool around you and linger longer at ground level. Therefore, I tend to set up my ambush spot/shots slightly farther than when elevated. I love close shots… but not too close. When in a treestand I'll normally position my shot distances at 12 to 15 yards. When in a ground blind, I tend to try for 15 to 20 yards because of lingering residual ground scent pooling.

Ground hunting is much tougher after the foliage drops and/or the frost kills the understory. Yes, you can see much better but so can they. No matter when I ground hunt from an ambush, I am always using the structure of the terrain to my advantage. One must be aware of slight deer movement variations dependent on the time of the day and time of the season. For example, if you have a thick, brushy creek bottom with an open or semi-open pasture adjacent to it running towards a bedding area/ridge, you'll find in the early season deer will tend to walk the open pasture rather than the thicker stuff even with similar wind directions. And especially in the mornings on their way between feeding and bedding areas. Think about it, it's just common sense. Rather than bull their way through the thick, wet briars and weeds heavy with the morning dew (and especially if they're running late from the crop field) they'll much prefer to slip up through the pasture quickly and quietly where going is easier, quieter, quicker and they can see better, scent-checking it just as well and still they're a jump or two away from heavy cover. Therefore, we have to set up accordingly. After the first frosts kill the leafy understory, the deer using those same basic morning patterns will adjust their movement from the pasture back into the thicker growth for security reasons. It all makes perfect sense and we must adapt to it.

If you have to set up in the heavy weeds and understory, you can increase usage where you want them to go by previously clipping trails by hand with a sickle or weed whacker to dictate where you want them to pass.

In the early season, the edge of a standing corn field is often a great ambush spot and is usually heavy with early scrapes. Although most of these scrapes are usually hit during the night, you may catch increased activity enroute to the bedding areas. Sitting in the woods looking out to the cornfield edge is one option with proper winds. But also, consider (wind directions pending) sitting right in the uncut cornfield itself. You'll be surprised at what you can get away with by sitting a half dozen or so rows deep. Picking your ambush location will vary greatly on the density of the cornstalks. Because the first few rows of the standing cornstalks will tend to be poor because of earlier heavy edge browsing, you may need to get in deeper. Try to find a spot where you can see them coming before they're right in your lap. Another little trick, instead of taking the path of least resistance by walking right along the edge of the cornfield, consider cutting the leaves from the standing stalks a few rows inward with a big knife or machete. This will give you a quiet approach even in dry, standing corn. Plus, you won't be as visible to any deer in the edge timber if it's already daylight. Additionally, you'll also not leave any residual ground scent on the edge of the field where the deer will surely be walking.

We also should think ahead. Knowing the corn will be cut later in the season after we've already had a couple killing frosts that thin out the understory, the deer will be shifting their field edge movement deeper into the timber similar to the pasture shift we just talked about. Prepare yourself an ideal ambush spot well in advance so it's all ready to slip into when its time.

You might want to consider even shifting their movement to your ambush spot by some selective cutting, such as a hinge-cut tree. Obviously, you only do this on your own property or with permission from the landowner. By cutting a six to eight-inch diameter tree partially through the trunk it will hopefully survive by still drawing enough moisture and nutrients up from the soil in order to keep it growing. If you are skilled enough to drop the tree at the proper angle, you can create a minor blockage to the deer's travel pattern shifting him closer to your ambush site.

Entrance/ exit to your ambush is a vital aspect of ground hunting. A quiet approach taking consideration in trying not to jump or disturb surrounding deer is imperative. Walk down in a dry or shallow creek bed if possible. Dry creek beds are a common but often overlooked hotspot for deer activity when the acorns are falling. Most tributaries will be lined with mature oaks because of the increased moisture in the bottoms. The big oaks will drop acorns where they will roll down the banks to be deposited in the creek bed itself. They'll accumulate just like a feed trough. A quick, hard rain will often wash them into little pools of "sweet spots." Trust me, all the deer know this.

Walking up and down the dry creek will locate the heavier usage. Bear in mind deer will be walking up and down the creek bed. But you can double your pleasure if you can find a heavy deposit of acorns near an established creek crossing. That way you can establish an ambush for deer walking crossways as well as deer walking up and down the creek itself. I often look for log jams within the creek beds near these spots. The same thing though, you have to be very aware of winds when down in these creek bed ambush spots. It's often hard to find one where the drifting winds are consistent. But if you do, these spots will afford you established cover within the creek itself and ideally give you a less distinct profile and sometimes even letting you peak up over the shelf. I've found creek drainages in wider valleys tend to have more consistent winds. A tributary between two steep side ridges will make winds very hard to depend on consistently and you'll be forced to deal with "slow walkers" becoming runners.

As stated, I try to always set up my ambush according to terrain structures. If the ridge lines are too steep for wind consistency, consider going uphill to normal shelfing on the ridges above the bottoms. Focus on pinch-points, headers (where eroded seepages begin). Wherever, I am most concerned with keeping a low profile and the wind consistencies.

One must always consider backlighting. VERY important. When setting up I prefer to have some cover both in front of me as well as behind me but cover behind me is more important in my opinion. Put 75% of the cover behind you and 25% in front of you. Put your back against a tree, a logjam or an embankment. Kick out the leaves to expose bare dirt for your feet. Break out your pruners and clip off a few cedar or pine boughs (or palmettos if down south) and stick them in front and/or behind you as needed. I'll often also just cut me out a hole at the base of an evergreen tree and back in, then pile the cuttings in front and behind me.

The bottom line is hunting on the ground is a superb thrill. Yes, hunting from an elevated position will likely let you kill more big, mature bucks. But sometimes as we get older, we must adapt to various situations where it's not all bad. One of the scariest parts is watching a huge buck blink at eye level.

Your chest will pound, and your heart will be in your throat. But, quite frankly, I can't think of many better circumstances for cardiac arrest.

"Deer do not have the ability to reason, but they can and will make judgement calls based on remembered information."

CHAPTER V
FRONT ROW SEAT

You may find throughout a lot of my writings over the years, some of the material I've shared repeatedly. I apologize for being repetitious but the fact remains it doesn't hurt to drum some of these opinions into our heads over and over. It's similar to highlighting a book. Yes, you've already read the part you're highlighting, but you're underlining it because it's important and you want to remember it. Therefore, I've left some repetitive parts throughout these books purposely.

For example, it's my opinion a buck doesn't hit his true trophy potential until full maturity. Notice I said "full" maturity. I don't think a buck is fully mature unless he's at least 5.5 years old. That includes even world-class bucks like the world record typical Milo Hansen buck from Saskatchewan, Canada. I was told Milo's buck was professionally aged and verified to be only 4.5 years old. That means although that buck was bigger than any buck in the world it likely would have been even bigger a year later. He probably would have had a very similar main frame but gained some mass, and likely would have gotten smarter and measured bigger.

After a buck reaches five and a half years of survival, he has pretty much learned all the ropes in his area. He's learned to use his territory and terrain to his advantage. He's also learned to use other deer in his area to his advantage. He's learned to depend on certain wind directions, to adjust his daily movements accordingly, become aware of the fact certain bedding areas and travel corridors are more secure than others. He's been educated to situations and various conditions within his world or he wouldn't still be alive. That woods-wise knowledge coupled with his natural senses is what makes him such a worthy challenge, especially for such close-range encounters.

I've always been a believer when hunting mature bucks, you are better off letting them come to you. That alone suggests setting up a situation and letting the proper scenario unfold. And that usually dictates proper treestand placement.

I choose my treestand locations according to multiple factors. I consider the time of the year; food sources; crop rotations; the pre-rut, rut or post-rut; AM versus PM, versus all-day; my entrance/exit; area hunting and/or other pressures; weather patterns; leaf-drop in the fall; water sources and consistent, dependable wind directions. It all adds up.

I personally think when you are showing someone the reasoning behind your decision on why you picked that very spot, you should be able to point out a dozen reasons to validate your decision on why you're there. Let's just touch on some of the variables.

SEPTEMBER AND EARLY OCTOBER:

I'm then basically hunting their food sources, or traveling to and from them. Although I'm not against it, I tend not to hunt directly in food plots. As of right now, I've never killed a deer in a food plot. The reason being mostly because I tend to hunt around plots rather than in/on them. I do use some food plots but I mostly use hidden plots more so to keep deer less visible to human traffic and to help them nutritionally during lean times. I much prefer to set myself up internally between their bedding and feeding areas. I believe mature deer feel much safer internally before exposing themselves to the vulnerable open conditions of a food plot. Therefore, I set up my ambush accordingly. Consider the overhead tree canopy, foliage densities, light intensities, food preferences, etc. Mature bucks tend to prefer the darker, cooler shadows of shaded areas. It's only common sense. When the foliage of the overhead canopy is thin where lush vegetation dominates the understory, a big buck doesn't have to move much. He just gets up from his bed and begins feeding or snacking. Early season temperatures tend to be hot. His coat is thickening whereas moving greater distances will overheat him. The shade/shadows will not only hide him but keep him cool.

If the weather has been hot or especially dry, pay very close attention to available water, especially if you have a hidden waterhole surrounded by dense cover. These areas can be real magnets in the early season and maybe only the early season. A friend of mine once killed a good buck in the prairie of eastern Montana at a seepage he found that held little more than maybe a bucket of water. But… it was the only available water for miles around. Most folks don't realize how important water is to most critters, especially during hotter temps. Most don't realize this because a lot of game will only visit water sources after dark. I'm not talking about a river or creek specifically. I'm talking a small pond or seepage in the open. Most game will be reluctant to water in daylight because they know they are more vulnerable through being visible, whereas they feel safer under the cover of darkness. But these examples all depend on the situation, location, density and cover surrounding the water/pond.

This is also the time of year to hunt mast crops at preferred locations discovered through scouting. Just as certain girls are sweeter than others, certain trees will bear better tasting, sweeter acorns than others. Maybe we better not go there! You'll only increase your close confrontations by isolating which are the "sweet oaks." You should be able to tell which trees are preferred due to the increased sign. Bank on it!

Speaking of "banks" don't overlook creek beds. Any seepage, whether dry or with a little water, will usually have an eroded bank due to previous high-water flow. If you pay attention, you'll usually notice more and bigger mature oaks due to increased moisture and rich soils along the creek bank. They may also be bigger oaks because of their position along the banks of the creek, where harvesting those trees might have been too difficult in the old days of logging.

You'll also notice when these nut-laden trees drop their crop the acorns will roll down the angled sides of the creek banks depositing concentrations of feed in the creek bed, very similar to a food trough. Trust me, the deer are aware of this and concentrate their search for sweet nuts in the dry creek itself. Again, it's only common sense. Moisture and rich soils promote fertile tree growth; gravity rolls the round acorns downhill; recent rains tend to wash out fallen foliage to expose a sand or gravel creek bottom laden with a mast crop of desirable acorns and nuts in a single concentration where they are easier to see and smell/find. It's a conglomeration of many factors that God granted us, along with our abilities to reason, in order to be stewards of the lands and wildlife. Yes, it may just be a seasonal opportunity but you can "bank" on it (no pun intended.)

Certain trees will hold their foliage longer than others. I've purposely done that before, where I'll ribbon off a certain tree in Late December that is still holding its leaves when all the other hardwoods have already shed their foliage months ago. Then, the following season I'll go to that ribboned tree knowing it will hold its cover longer.

When picking a tree for a late fall stand location always take leaf-drop into consideration. Some hardwood trees that would make perfectly fine ambush locations in September and/or October will be out of the question once the leaves fall. So, we must also consider present backlighting versus what the backlighting will be like after leaf-drop.

The same is true if the background holds a distant dark ridge in one spot and open sky for a background in the next. Sometimes I'll purposely keep my stand height low in order to take advantage of a darker, distant background ridge, rather than a stand six feet higher in the same tree where you would lose that distant back-drop advantage. Always remember backlighting is vitally important in keeping an inconspicuous profile. With a proper hunting wind direction, I'd much rather be elevated only ten feet and have a good dark background, than be elevated twenty feet with backlighting.

LATE OCTOBER AND ALL OF NOVEMBER:

Simply stated, my main method of operation is I hunt terrain/structure to take advantage of natural movement, whether during the rut or not. We need to prepare ourselves mentally to the fact big, mature bucks WILL be on the move. A lot of it is positive thinking. Your stand positioning has been predetermined to be THE best option for that particular time/day. We must convince ourselves that if we've done our homework properly there's no other place that would be more productive. Simply stated, scouting creates confidence; confidence gives us patience; patience offers opportunity, and opportunity hopefully leads to success. It's just a matter of time.

Terrain and structure will dictate movement year after year. Yes, things change annually, but the terrain itself usually takes many decades in order to alter movement patterns. When I refer to terrain, I am likely talking about the earth itself. Whereas, when I'm talking structure, I may be referring to obstructions like deadfalls and/or downed trees or understory densities. Selective logging is a good example. After a block of timber is selectively logged, trees may fall into locations that will absolutely change the travel patterns the local deer have dealt with their whole lives. New obstacles arise. It may take several years (2 or 3) for the deer to try the new structures forcing differences in movement patterns. The smart land manager will take this into consideration BEFORE the selective logging so he can have those same trees dropped to his advantage. In other words, drop the trees so they will fall to the benefit of the hunter rather than the deer.

Hunting concentrated pinch-points within security cover will eventually produce action for you. Develop the mindset the longer you cover these areas under ideal conditions it's just a matter of time until your opportunity arises. Rather than think, "I've been sitting at this spot for eight hours and still haven't seen the big one" ... think instead, "I've been sitting at this spot for eight hours and still haven't seen the big one...but... that means I'm closer to the time he passes than I was when I started." Think positive rather than negative. If you should consider leaving for no good reason, remember this... the longer you sit in that pre-determined, well thought out location the closer you are to the time when that big buck who made all that sign in front of you will be back. Will him in!

Again, being repetitious, be aware foliage is dropping now and the canopy is opening up. The understory is also thinning and will alter security movement. Early season lush, thick ground vegetation will alter deer movements. Again, it's just common sense. A deer travels from feeding to bedding each morning. In September and early October, the understory is thick and wet from morning dew. He's forced to deal with vines and briars, etc. If a buck has a relatively open pasture he can slip through, (especially if he happens to be running late in the morning) and especially if it's just a jump or two away from security cover, he'll often gamble exposing himself for a minute or two to cover some open ground quickly, rather than bulling his way through chest deep, wet understory and stickers. Again, it's just common sense. After the first hard frost and the understory opens up, he will then often opt for the more secure cover within the timber rather than the pasture short-cut. We must adjust ourselves accordingly.

LATE NOVEMBER THROUGH JANUARY:

The rut is basically finished. I now again start hunting to and from the food sources, or the food itself because nutrition now becomes vitally important. Remember the foliage has now opened up to a degree you will be much more visible in the hardwoods, both while in the stand and on entrance/exit. Yes, you can see better but so can they. If it's daylight when you climb into the stand a deer will watch you get into position from a long way off. And he'll remember it and avoid the area.

Backlighting here, if standing on the ground, would create a solid blob, which wouldn't look normal to a passing deer. Being elevated only four feet up, with the light passing beneath, creates an entirely different picture for the deer.

Yes, there will still be some late rutting action. Any does that were not successfully impregnated will again come into heat a month after the peak rut. Also, some young does will also enter their first cycle and perfume the air. This, in itself, will stimulate some action, so don't be surprised if you see the biggest buck of the season now.

At this time, I tend to choose softwood trees to hunt from. Consider cedars, junipers and pines since they don't shed their needles like leaves and will afford much better cover for the treestand hunter. Locating a good tree in the right location is the trick. Don't worry about stand elevation so much. I'd much

Sometimes a situation dictates a low stand

rather be elevated only 8 or 10 feet in a thick softwood tree than twenty feet up in an open hardwood that looks like a telephone pole. I've killed some giant bucks with my bow when my feet were only eight feet above ground level.

I have morning stands, evening stands and all-day stand

options. I also have stands set up for various winds and only hunt them when everything is perfect.

I like to have plenty of options so I can rotate positions and not over-hunt any particular area. I try not to "taint" an area by over-hunting it unless it's a special situation. And normally I won't hunt from the same stand two days in a row.

I try to vary my entrance/exit according to wind directions so they don't hopefully pattern me. I tend to force myself to walk a long way under the cover of darkness so as not to educate deer to my presence with the noise of a vehicle.

I walk in/out when it's dark. When it's dark a deer thinks it's invisible, You can get away with a lot more visually when its dark than you can when it's light out. But ALWAYS be aware of the wind directions and any shifting.

Do NOT hunt a stand no matter how good it seems if the wind is not right. They WILL nail you and you'll alter their patterns for weeks or even the rest of the season. Deer DO... I repeat... deer DO remember! Don't think for a minute your invasive intrusion won't alter their patterns for weeks.

I personally like to have a lot of stand options pre-hung before the season in order to capitalize on a sneaky approach additional to the reasons listed above. If the hunter doesn't have the number of different stands available, i.e., on public land, he can at least erect multiple stand sites, have them all detailed and trimmed prior to the season and replace them accordingly when needed. Hang your stand when it's right but make sure to keep your disturbances to a minimum or you'll defeat the whole purpose.

Plan your hunt and hunt your plan. Be sneaky. If you're lucky, God will give you a great front row seat for the show.

CHAPTER VI
FROM AN OWL TO A CAT

I've always considered sitting in a treestand very similar to an owl on a perch watching for movement. In the same respect, I've also always considered any cat the epitome of a still-hunter/stalker. I've been of the opinion when bowhunting for fully mature whitetails you are better off letting them come to you rather than vice versa. First, I again want to clarify I am speaking fully mature whitetails.

The difference is both physical and psychological between a 4.5 and a 5.5-year-old deer. I've always been of the opinion a buck needs to be at least 5.5 years old to reach his first true TROPHY potential. As nice as he is at 4.5, if given one more year he'll almost always be bigger. No offence intended for those who take an outstanding 4.5-year-old, but it seems a shame to not let a great buck reach his full physical potential. But as I stated, there are circumstances that absolutely vary and to each his own regarding the outcome.

I also believe that each animal has a specific, unique personality and psychological makeup. I believe their individual intelligence is derived additionally from survival experiences gained each year as they get older and more mature. The more times they face adversity, the smarter they become. It's nature's way. Only the strong (smart or lucky) will survive. It's survival of the fittest for perpetuity of the species. Each year adds multiple conflicts in a world of survival. They are forced to adapt in order to live. Plain and simple, they learn to improve via their instincts. What is often thought of as reasoning is actually nothing but instinctiveness. They learn to use other deer and their surroundings to their advantage. They absolutely remember. Their very existence depends on it.

On the other side of the equation, be it birds of prey, felines or canines, all predators must also adapt in the predator/prey "game" of survival. If they don't, they too will die. It's serious business.

With hunters, the outcome of a day in the timber might be momentous but it's not as significant in our survival. I have purposely accepted the relative close-range limitations of my chosen weapons as a distinct disadvantage in my pursuit. It's a primal game that challenges me to the core. Not to get philosophical, it's been rightly stated we kill in order to have hunted.

Similar to an old buck, age has made me slow down. In some ways it's disheartening because my physical capabilities cannot keep up with my mental cravings. On the other hand, I feel like I'm hunting smarter than I did in my youth. And my results with big, fully mature bucks in the last decade pretty much proves me right.

So, when it comes to success on mature bucks, I let them come to me at a well thought out, predetermined ambush site. I get a huge amount of satisfaction studying terrain, putting together all the pieces for predictability and then taking or passing a trophy buck just like I knew the scenario would eventually play out.

One of the primary ingredients to success is hunting undisturbed deer. Undisturbed animals offer some predictability in their normal movements. This, along with the increased "normal" activities of the rut, will add up to our best chance for opportunity.

Some people think I have sole hunting rights on great private properties. I don't really. Although I tend to concentrate my hunting efforts on five farms with limited access, I don't have exclusivity on any one farm... none. Nor do I own a single acre I can call my own. I've never hunted or killed a deer on my own property in my life. I wish it were different but it's not.

I'm a big believer in monitoring your hunting properties as part of property management. Patrolling properties is an unfortunate part of keeping some individuals honest. It's a good idea to let outsiders know your property is monitored both externally and internally with motion activated cameras 24/7. Additionally, the purposeful presence of a parked vehicle when carefully hunting the fringes will let the bad guys know your farm hasn't been abandoned. In the same respect, while still trying to be a "nice guy", make sure everyone knows you have full intentions to prosecute trespassers to the full extent of the law... without any exceptions. No second chances... ever. Sorry to say if you let one trespasser go with only a warning, he'll spread the word you're easy and I'll guarantee it'll bring you more headaches. They know they are wrong. I've caught them red-handed. They'll look you right in the eye and lie to your face. You have to let them know you are serious about this stuff... very serious.

Back in the '90s I used to hunt/guide on the Milk River of eastern Montana. The ranch controlled several miles of bottoms on both sides of the river. It had not been gun hunted since 1967 if I remember correctly. I found it very interesting that you could hunt adjoining properties which were gun hunted and easily see the difference in the demeanor of the resident deer.

When deer were disturbed on the gun hunted farms, they had obvious fear in their eyes. Comparatively, when deer were disturbed in the bowhunting-only area, fear was replaced with aggravation. They displayed behavior like we were just annoying them and shifted accordingly. We were more of a nuisance, a pain in the butt to them than a genuine threat.

Since the Milk River divided the ranch longitudinally you could take a patch of timber that was historically better rut hunting in November and purposely disturb sections across, upriver or down river making the prime piece even better during the rut. Deer would actually shift their daytime rut activities into less disturbed areas. It's all just common sense. Undisturbed trumps disturbed.

Some years I'll use my October hunting to find and learn new turf in order to lessen the impact on my rut areas, playing the odds so to speak. Beautiful Indian-Summer type balmy weather and peak fall foliage colors come with subdued deer movement. Deer don't have to move much between bedding and feeding. They just arise from their beds, take a few steps and start feeding. So, a plan is needed to take advantage of the situation.

Think about it. Everything pretty much goes against stand hunting options. The foliage is thick so we are unable to see longer ranges. This means when we do see something its likely substantially closer. But it also means they cannot see us as readily. Again, you don't want to disturb your best areas... they remember! The deer aren't moving as much anyway. Mast crop abundance and usage is at it's peak. It all suggests one option. Use this "down time" to switch from being an owl to being a cat.

But be a smart cat. Don't just go for a walk in the woods. Use your head. This is a perfect time to check out some secondary areas, regions/farms that will not FOR NOW be detrimental when slightly disturbed. Your finding might turn up a honey-hole you can capitalize on in the future. But most importantly we must hunt with a plan.

Just like any other situation there will be some days that are better than others. I prefer cloudy days. A good cloud cover will block sunline, not making it too "hot" (bright) and lessen shadows. Deer use shadows and light intensities every day in their movements to survive. We, as hunters, should as well. If there are shadows or darker/shaded areas along your path, learn to use them to your advantage. Slip shadow to shadow if possible. But very slowly cross lighted areas knowing you will be in the bright sunlight with your movement exaggerated.

My definition of still-hunting is more or less being a mobile stand. Adjust your pace so you are hardly moving at all. Read that sentence again. Without getting into this too deeply right now, over the years we have been taught when still-hunting to look for the horizontal line of a deer's back or belly, a shiny eyeball, a white throat patch or the "V" of the tail. That's all well and good but I'm here to tell you to watch for MOVEMENT.

That's what they do. Learn to stare in stationary segments rather than scanning. Your eyes will pick up movement way sooner than scanning. If I'm in a treestand and have a deer within sight I'll always try to watch it undisturbed. They will pick up additional animals in the distance way before I will. Depend on it. Watch their body language. If they stare intently at something you better believe they saw some movement. It might have been a bird, a squirrel, a coon or whatever, but they are studying something and they likely first saw it because of movement. My point is it takes time for us to pick out the distant flick of an ear or the flip of a tail. We must slow down when still-hunting in order to catch these things. One of the best tips I ever got regarding still-hunting was to walk into the area quietly and slowly you intend to still-hunt. Then LIE DOWN on the ground and close your eyes and listen intently. Listen until you finally hear something fairly close to your position. Then, open your eyes and slowly roll to your feet and picture yourself as the prey. Imagine something is hunting for you and you need to slowly... very slowly get out of the area without being detected. Do this ritual in order to get yourself into the proper mind-frame for still-hunting. Once at this point you then convert from hunted to hunter.

Slowing your pace will give you time to think and become one with nature. Did you ever notice deer will pick up horizontal movements quicker than vertical movements? I went over this in detail elsewhere in a chapter on eyes, but I wanted to mention the importance of being aware of this again here. Try to maintain vertical movements.

I love to still-hunt in the rain. I'm not talking about a downpour but a slow, quiet rain is fine with me. A heavy mist is even better. The understory is wet. The ground leaves turn to soggy cornflakes. A heavy rain is miserable so most deer will be holed up. But a slight drizzle will have a lot of game moving around, especially right after a storm-front moves through. The heavy rain will subside and a mist or slight drizzle will continue. This is often the trigger that draws bedded deer into freely moving.

An observant woodsman will also notice deer tend to bed in the open when the woods are wet both during and after a rain.

They'll often bed in a CRP or weed field rather than the timber. At first one would think, "why would they do that? Why wouldn't they be curled up under a pine tree in the rain?" The answer is very logical. If they are bedded in the timber their visibility is limited; the wind is blowing the cover all around them; everything is moving; the raindrops are dropping onto the ground-leaves making a constant dripping noise. They can't hear or see defensively as well. Whereas, if they bed in an open weed field, they can see around themselves better; there's less movement of overhanging limbs blowing in the wind; and there's no constant dripping of water drops hitting the ground cover. It's quieter and they can see better. Look for them there.

If it's slightly raining or just recently stopped, I accept the fact I am going to get wet. When it's quiet I'd just as soon leave the rain gear at home because it's too noisy in my opinion. But if it's really windy background noise might cover any raincoat noise. But if it's quiet I'll just wear either wool or polar fleece at less risk.

Air temps will help me decide whether wool or fleece is better. If it's a warm rain, the polar fleece might be a little cooler than wool. But if it's a cold rain I prefer the warmer, insulating effects of the wool. When wool is literally saturated it's usually heavier in weight than fleece. But the fact wool has natural lanolin usually prevents it from complete saturation over fleece.

Proper footwear when still-hunting is imperative. I usually wear rubber bottoms/ leather tops. Just make sure you keep away from the lug-type soles used in rocky terrain. Lugs are too thick and stiff normally. Although, if you are still-hunting in steeper terrain on wet or muddy slopes the sharper edge of the boot sole might dig in the hillside better and keep you from sliding too much. But normally lug soles are too thick and stiff. You can't "feel" the ground with them. The late/great, legendary bowhunter Paul Schafer from Montana used to wear knee-high Indian moccasins that had a double layered leather, untreaded sole. He only wore them when stalking in dry weather that wasn't too steep or slippery and also where ankle support wasn't a big issue. When it was warm and wet, he often wore a heavy wool sock, then a pair of thin, black, stretchy pull-on shoe/boot rubbers over the wool socks; then he'd put a second pair of over-sized gray wool socks over the rubbers. This combination would be really quiet, still keep your feet dry and let you feel the ground well. Obviously, you wouldn't wear this combo if you were hunting near heavy thorns or cactus., etc.

I don't know if it's my imagination, but it sure seems like we've been getting more than our share of high winds in the last several years. I'm talking 25 MPH winds with even higher gusts. Some deer will get down into draws or on the leeward/downwind side of slopes to try to escape the higher winds. Some will take shelter in a pine/cedar thicket when it's excessively cold and windy. When temperatures are not too severe and crops are still standing, they'll often take shelter right within the rows of an unharvested cornfield.

Close inspection will also show, similar to bedding on the leeward side of a ridge, they will tend to bed on the downwind side of a standing cornfield, especially where the rows of planted crops are perpendicular to the direction the wind is blowing, rather than the rows and wind direction being parallel. Wind blowing crosswise to the planted rows let each row of standing stalks act as a baffle. And you'll normally find more deer bedding on that downwind side of the field. Note, these examples are in high wind situations. When it's normal wind velocities they might bed with parallel or perpendicular directions but on the downwind ends. It's all just common sense that we humans normally never think about, yet the whitetails adjust to daily.

Modern farming techniques with more narrow corn rows and stalks planted closer together might be better for the deer but aren't as good for the still-hunter. Up until the late '80s, or so, you could frequently find corn rows wide enough to walk down without having to bull your way through. They were often wide enough to offer substantial weed growth between the corn rows. These little weedy areas/patches were magnets for deer to bed in securely. A still-hunter could catch a favorable wind and stalk across the length of the corn rows, perpendicular to the rows, often catching a buck bedded at ultra-close range.

Just take a single row at a time, looking both ways before you proceed to the next row. If you see one bedded, try to quickly determine which way he is facing/bedded. Obviously, using the wind to your advantage, you sometimes may need to drop back the way you came in for a couple rows. Then swing wide and try to approach from behind him where his peripheral vision is best for your advancement. This technique works best on a windy day. The noise of dry standing corn leaves blowing in the wind covers any normally loud approach. Not to mention, the still-

Corn provides security for deer

hunter will be walking on previously tilled-up dirt rather than fallen, dry foliage or rocks/gravel.

We need to plan our days carefully. I like to plan my hunt and hunt my plan. I don't just go for a "walk in the woods." I've covered this somewhat elsewhere before but I'm going to touch on it again because of its importance.

When I go into a new area, the first thing I usually do is follow any creek bottoms or drainages. They don't even need to have water in them necessarily. I'm studying the terrain/contours, not looking for water. By walking the drainages longitudinally, you can locate the best crossings. This will give you a starting point to learn about the area as well as giving you some direction for your best still-hunting.

I often use this technique of still-hunting while at the same time scouting new turf. Depending on my findings I may want to branch out from there to follow seepages while learning specific terrain structures.

This same line of thinking is used to plan a day's still-hunting. If you think about it, you'll realize it's again nothing but common sense. The creek bottoms and drainages are in the valleys where gravity pulls water downward. The increased moisture in the bottoms tend to be more conducive for both understory/plant and tree growth. In a normal hardwood bottom you'll normally find better soil nutrients because of sedimentation. Increased nutrients result in bigger, healthier, more mature trees. Also, if you are dealing with mast producing trees it will concentrate a desired food source in a focused area. This is where you want to still-hunt.

Now, think about it even more. These are "pieces of the puzzle" you want to take in while you're slowly slipping along. Here we go... thinking again! Look closely at the drainage itself. First, how wide is the valley? A bottom that is a hundred yards or more wide will have a lot more stable wind drifts than one in a tight valley floor.

Next, look at the depth of the creek bottom itself as compared to the flat shelf just above the creek bed. The approximate height of a mature deer's eyelevel is only between three and four feet. If the creek bed is shallow, a deer can walk right in the creek bed itself, down over the lip, remaining less obvious (out of sight) and still be able to see up over the lip onto the flats paralleling the creek for any disturbances.

If the creek is deeper than eye level of a deer, he'll be walking blindly. Therefore, he'll shift his travel pattern up onto the shelf itself in order to walk parallel to the main drainage.

Now, he'll be able to look down into the creek rather than be looking up out of it. Again, common sense will dictate how he moves to maintain efficiency and safety. We must use our God-given ability to reason in order to learn what nature takes for granted. And we must adjust our hunting techniques accordingly to be more productive.

Still maintaining our feline techniques, next consider our "rite of passage." Even if the creek bed is dry, or mostly dry, there will usually be fewer leaves littering the ground. Recent, previous rains will have washed a lot of them away. This results in fewer, dead, dry leaves to slip through. Also note the soil types and adjust your travel accordingly. Soft, sandy soil, clay or solid mud will obviously be much quieter to walk in/on than rocks or gravel. If the creek has water in it, often noise of the babbling brook will cover your intrusion. You should be walking slow enough to avoid any sounds of a human gait. Although I've never gone that far, I understand some still-hunters will actually drag a small branch on a cord behind them in order for the noise to eliminate any cadence to their gait. Probably not a bad idea.

Fall mast droppings will concentrate acorns along AND in the creek itself. Here, common sense tells us mature trees along the creek bank drop their nuts straight down. If the acorn doesn't drop on the shelf above the creek, gravity will result in it rolling down into the creek bed itself. This makes them easier to find for the deer rather than having to scrounge through six inches of dry leaves. The nuts will concentrate right on the open, sandy/gravel flats of the creek bed itself, making them much easier to locate. Deer know this... trust me.

With this information you can plan your October still-hunt

accordingly. You now know where the prime food source is concentrated and therefore, you know where you'll have a better chance of locating your game. Don't stop reasoning yet. Now you need to plan your approach. A lot will depend on the width of the valley and the depth of the creek itself. Remember, if the creek depth (not water depth) is shallow the deer will likely be right down in the creek bed. You only really have one choice here since they can and will be watching the flats above the creek. Hopefully the creek will have multiple twists and turns slowing you to still-hunt according to the best wind direction. In this case, your chances are now 50/50 the feeding animals will be working either towards you or away from you. If he's coming your way merely backtrack a little in order to set up and ambush him when he comes around the bend. If he's moving away from you, either wait him out hoping he'll turn (they often do) or you can backtrack and, depending on the terrain and winds, possibly loop in front of him and hope for the best.

This brings us to the situation of how we should still-hunt the bottom if the creek bed is deeper than a standing deer's eye level. Knowing many fallen acorns have rolled down into the creek and the deer's eye height is not able to see up over the shelf, the best approach will be a "stitching" effect. Quietly slip in from above with the winds obviously in your favor until you can see up or downstream enough to verify any activity. If nothing is present you backtrack slowly to make another stitch or loop that will oversee virgin creek beds. Should you see deer,

In the timber

you now have a couple options to choose from and it'll usually depend on the situation. The first step is to try to determine the animal's direction of travel. If he is coming in your direction an ambush is possible. If he's not, you have the option to swing/loop ahead of him and possibly set up another ambush. But here's where you need to make an important decision. Always be aware because of the prey's superior senses, you'll often get busted. Realize if you do get busted, the spooked animal will likely disturb the entire area. So, your choices are to either let the situation play out, back off, or go for it. Decisions... decisions.

A similar plan is used when still-hunting ridges. Don't just go for a walk. Yes, a nice autumn walk is aesthetically pleasing, but if we have a master plan, we will greatly increase our odds for success. Knowing deer tend to bed on the leeward side of a ridge with the winds at their backs and thermal drifts in their faces, a stitching or looping travel pattern is possible if wind angles are considered and consistent. But these situations all vary and should only be considered with no variations in wind directions and travel patterns (to/from food sources). It can be done but it's really rare and tough even when we adapt.

Open hardwoods will dictate extremely slow movement. If you're forced to wade through briar thickets you might want to consider the fact if you're wearing a ghillie suit you'll be dealing with snagging. Two items I always have with me when still hunting are a good pair of binoculars and a pair of ratchet hand pruners (I like the Florian brand best.) The binoculars are used almost constantly for picking out detail before you advance. Just this suggestion alone will force you to slow your pace. A still-hunter can't be moving forward much when constantly using glasses to scan ahead. The pruners help you to cut the best path. I guarantee you will sooner or later come to a situation where you will have the option to go around an obstacle of brush creating unnecessary movement or quietly snipping your way through it.

If the understory is not too thick, I much prefer still-hunting with a ghillie suit, although I'm of the opinion a lot of Ghillie suits tend to be too dark when viewed from a distance. I've mentioned before I purposely only wear the three-quarter length coat. This is also done for a reason. The three-quarter length is enough to blend your upright torso into the understory while lessening the drag of snagging. If I should come to a log or stump I might want to sit on, the three-quarter length will cover my sitting legs all the way to the ground. I also opted for the

I foolishly passed this buck at 15 yards on the groun because it was too early in the season and I didn't want to tag out. Dang!

lightweight version as some ghillies tend to be quite heavy/warm. Because you are mostly mobile you are keeping your circulation going, plus October still-hunting tends to be warmer anyway. Go lightweight, you can layer it if needed.

Most importantly regarding a ghillie suit, I always wear the ghillie hat. I'm of the opinion that the hat is by far the most important part of the outfit. The shaggy strips that hang down from the circular, full hat brim will totally eliminate the dreaded human head sitting atop human shoulders.

I always go with complete camo. That includes a facemask, gloves or hand-paint as well.

Another thing to consider is fletching colors if bowhunting. When I first started filming my bowhunts I went with solid

The ghillie suit works!

yellow feathers coupled with solid yellow arrow cresting in hopes the human eye could follow the flight of the arrow on film. This seemed to work fine from a treestand since I normally remove my bow quiver from the bow when elevated. But, when on the ground still-hunting and moving, a "block" of bright yellow feathers/cresting is too obvious and easily detected when in motion. Therefore, either go with barred, less obvious fletching colors, or use a fletch hood/cover.

Often in late October you'll be slipping along, when all of a sudden you'll be confronted by a doe that might have prematurely come into heat, with a buck or three in hot pursuit. You'll be treated to a front row seat. Accept it with a smile, as an offering. But remember, it'll never happen if you don't try.

The whole concept is to silently, slowly drift from shadow to shadow until the proper scenario presents itself. Make yourself into a mobile stand. Gear down your mobility but move with a purpose and direction. After some pre-season scouting gives you an area with some confidence of success, put together a plan and transform yourself from being an owl to a cat. The rewards can be tremendous.

> *"Establish a good strategy based upon terrain structure in areas known to produce big bucks. Set the situation up and only hunt it undisturbed, under optimal conditions that are to your advantage."*

Looking for movement!

CHAPTER VII
NOW EYE GET IT

I'd like to relay some hunting opinions you likely have not heard before. They will make you a better hunter with either a rifle or a bow.

When I was only about seven or eight years old, I distinctly remember my Dad teaching me some whitetail wisdom that I'd like to hand down to you at this time. Dad was a great whitetail hunter in his own right. He died prematurely in an accident at the early age of 44. Until then, I remember him complaining somewhat about other hunters following him in the timber because he always got the action. Looking back on it, I do think a lot of his "luck" was just natural ability.

You have to realize this was in the late 1940s and 1950s. There were really not many sources of hunting information or knowledge available back then. There were the "big three" hunting magazines, which included, Outdoor Life, Sports Afield and Field and Stream. But almost all whitetail articles within those publications were stories of successful hunts behind the barn, or an article featuring a specific hunting region or outfitter. They were all entertainment rather than educational pieces. My point is, I have no idea where Dad came up with his information, but I'm pretty sure it was self-taught… and the fact remains he was right/ spot on until today.

It seems these days everyone is looking for the big secret. I hate to be the one to break the news but there isn't any one big secret. Successful whitetail hunting is a conglomeration of a bunch of little secrets, of which most are derived from real, quality time spent in the timber. Time spent watching, listening and thinking. I repeat, time spent thinking about exactly what you are seeing. Sign lays there for all of us to educate ourselves for the future. Knowledge is power and we must never stop learning. The more you learn the small pieces of the puzzle, the more you'll see and understand the big picture and will be able to adapt accordingly.

For whatever reason, I distinctly remember Dad saying, "Remember this... if you have a whitetail you want to shoot standing broadside at twenty-five yards or under looking at you, if you raise your weapon (gun or bow) vertically (big boy talk for up and down) you have a chance. But, if you swing your weapon (gun or bow) horizontally (big boy talk for left to right or right to left) he'll bust you every time." So, if you slowly raise your weapon straight up and down, you'd likely be okay. But if you tried to move horizontally, such as the" swing-draw" method of shooting a bow, you'll learn why they call them whitetails.

Over the years I tested it and I found Dad to be absolutely right time after time. I just accepted that until just a few years ago. My inquisitive nature wanted to know why. Research showed me it had to do with the rods and cones in a deer's eyes. Bear with the scientific reasoning a little because we as humans/hunters have a lot to learn here.

The eyes of a predator

The rods in a deer's eyes are responsible for movement and light sensitivity. The cones are responsible for color perception and resolution. It makes absolute, perfect sense. Deer are a prey specie.

Being a prey species predators come at them horizontally.

The pupils of a prey species tend to lay horizontal in order to detect predators coming in horizontally. Think about it: almost all deer predators: coyotes, wolves, cougars, bobcats, dogs, bears, and humans all come at them horizontally. Whereas, most but not all predators tend to have vertical pupils. Notice the pupils on cats, owls, etc. Interesting? Yes. Coincidence? I think not.

How can we as hunters use this information? Think about it. Use your common sense of reasoning. We've all read when in the deer woods to look for the white throat patch; the white "V" of the tail; the flat/horizontal back or belly line of a standing whitetail. That's all fine, but what we must mostly look for is MOVEMENT. That's what the critters are looking for... movement. The flick of an ear or the twitch of a tail. In fact, that twitch of the white tail in deer language means everything is fine and dandy.

I lived in western Montana for almost thirty years. A lot of the old-time elk outfitters/guides would ride a pack string of horses miles back into the big country to set up spike camps. The seasoned pro-outfitter/guide wouldn't waste his time looking for elk. He'd watch his horse. When the horse picked up movement, he knew it. All of a sudden, the outfitter would point out there 800 yds. to a group of elk heading over the Divide. The hunters were impressed with the old boy when realistically they should have been giving the tip of the hat to the horse.

I've often been amused how some hunters think, or maybe I should say don't think. I've had guys say to me, "this little buck came right there 20 yards next to me and bedded down. I drew on him four times before he busted me." I ask myself, why would you keep drawing your bow on him until he busts you? Whenever I have a deer bed down close, I LOVE it. I can relax and just watch that bedded deer. They will pick up any incoming deer way before I will. And you'll know strictly from their body language what to expect.

So, how do we as predators/hunters use this knowledge to our benefit? Bear with me on this as it may be a little difficult to put into words. Say you are sitting in a treestand overlooking a valley of timber right in front of you. Or, in the gun hunter's example, say you top a ridgeline and are viewing the valley in front of you for the first time. In either example, most hunters will scan the valley ahead with our eyes swinging right and left. That's a major mistake in my opinion. This is where it gets hard to explain so bear with me. If you scan a ridge with your eyes and head moving left to right, you'll notice the background will appear to be moving right to left. It's similar to learning which of your eyes are dominant. Most right-handed people tend to be right-eye dominant. Point your finger at an object twenty feet away with both eyes open. If you are right-eye dominant you'll notice your finger will align with the object you are pointing at with your right eye. Now, close your right eye. You'll notice your finger suddenly seems to jump to the right and you'll now be looking parallel to your aiming/pointing finger and not right down it.

Bear with me. There's probably a scientific name for this but I'm not smart enough to relay it and it doesn't really matter. I'm pointing out (no pun intended) when you scan a ridgeline or valley in front of your face by moving your eyes and/or head scanning, you are having the background appear to move in the opposite direction you are scanning. Because the background appears moving you are much less likely to detect movement.

And, like I said previously, what we as predators want to look for is movement. That's very important.

So, when you are in your stand, or top a ridge, rather than fluid scanning for movement WE MUST LEARN TO SCAN IN INCREMENTS. Think about it. When a deer is scanning a field or valley in front of himself, he doesn't scan or rotate his head smoothly left and right. He looks at a single/specific spot looking for movement. Then, after a few seconds he will rotate his head a little either left or right, hold it still and stare again (looking for movement). This is how they survive, by looking for movement as they stare at one spot. This is why they are so much quicker to detect incoming deer than we are. It would behoove us to be more like them in this instance.

Another example to think about is that predators are the only critters, that I know of, that when running away from you will rotate their heads and look back over their shoulders at you, i.e. coyotes, wolves, dogs, etc. Prey animals don't do that. They run away, then stop, turn and look back over their shoulders. Our western mule deer are famous for this trait. And many hunters call them dumb for doing so. Interesting. You get my point.

Use this spot stare knowledge to your advantage whenever you hunt. Scanning is a hard habit to break but you will see a lot more deer if you train yourself to look in increments.

Another example for vertical/horizontal movement, say you hang a stand in a triangle of three mature trees so your stand sits in the middle of the triangle. Perfect, good cover around you. But most people will screw in a bow holder off to the side so their weapon won't be hanging in their way. Each situation varies but consider keeping your weapon more in front of you, if possible, rather than off to the side "out of the way". Because you'll be forced to swing your weapon horizontally (there we go again) rather than vertically from the bow hook when it's crunch time.

Use our God given talents to reason. Spend time in the woods. Slow down and think about what you are seeing. Study our wildlife because all is related. If you do so, you will appreciate your success more because it will be earned. You will have self-pride when you sit back and say to yourself, "Now EYE get it!

"Coyotes probably kill more big, fully mature trophy bucks than all the rest of the deer herd combined."

CHAPTER VIII
TIDBITS

I wanted to add this chapter of tidbits, some of which you may or may not already know. Please bear with the fact I might have already mentioned some of these variable short subjects within my previous writings. But also consider the fact that repeating them in more detail might be even more beneficial in case they didn't sink in deep enough the first time around.

First, a couple things. These are generalizations, so please accept them as that. They might vary depending on the years, locations, seasons, hunting pressures, latitudes/elevations, etc. These tidbits will not simply be black and white. Consider the fact these theories are NOT scientific, biological certainties. They are not much more than my own personal opinions. But also consider I've developed these opinions after many decades of learning and personally seeing examples via practical experiences in the timber. These are not "book learned" conclusions but are perceptions I've gained an understanding of via closer study than casual observing. This is yet another prime example of slowing down and thinking about what we are seeing.

TROLLING FOR A BUCK: Without getting into boring details the general timing of the rut is based on reproduction of the species and fawn survival rates. Due to the variable gestation periods, most of the breeding takes place in November, with slight variations in later October and December. This timing is specifically coordinated so fawns are not dropped too early in the spring, nor too late. Generally speaking, the bucks are pretty much always ready to breed when they have hard antlers.

Whereas, the does are not ready/ willing until it's time... (you guys probably know the feeling!)

Over the last sixty-plus years I've spent untold numbers of hours sitting in a treestand watching. I've witnessed this occurrence many times, as I'm sure other hunters have, but it's not often they realize what they are seeing. The best way to explain this is for me to portray a scenario where you can think back if you've ever seen this yourself.

Let's say you're sitting in a treestand three-quarters of the way up the side of a hardwood ridge. It's mid-November, so most of the foliage has dropped allowing you to see a good two hundred yards across the valley and the entire hillside across from you. All of a sudden movement catches your eye and you see a single, mature doe running fast with her tail up. She's running fast, like she's being pushed by something. You watch behind her expecting to see a buck following. But no bucks; maybe a coyote or another hunter. Nope, nothing.

All of a sudden, she slams on the brakes and stops for maybe five or ten seconds. Then she takes off again running up the mountain. Again, she stops for a short pause, then takes off again, this time swinging back in the direction you first saw her come from. Minutes later, here she comes again. You suddenly realize she is running a pattern of "sideways laying figure 8s". that are covering several hundred yards from left to right and back. You watch her and think, "look at that silly dimwit." She's running around the whole side of the mountain flagging her tail. Then, all of sudden it strikes you. What she's doing is she's TRYING to draw attention to herself! She's a hot doe and she's ready to be bred. There happens to not be any bucks around her on the ridge at that moment. She's TROLLING, plain and simple. THINK about what you're seeing. It makes perfect sense. Nature is cool!

WIND DETECTORS: Pretty much everyone knows we need to be aware of the wind directions for successful whitetail hunting. The sad fact is even though people might be generally aware of wind directions, not many realize the importance of us constantly needing to check for even minor changes/shifts. Over the years I've gone from wetting a finger; to lighting a match; a bottle of kid's toy bubbles with the hoop; a feather on a thread tied to the upper limb of your bow tip; warm breath on a cold morning; talcum powder in a puff bottle, etc. I've tried them all. The two I like the best I'll go over in detail. My second favorite is spun polyester yarn. You can buy it in bigger sporting goods stores and flyfishing shops usually. It often comes in bright colors i.e., chartreuse, blaze orange or hot pink. And you can also get it on the internet in lengths of 12 feet for $3. I cut the yarn into 6" lengths. I carry it either in the watch pocket of my pants or else tuck it in the upper corner of my right front pants pocket. That way it's easy to access and always right there. As soon as I get into my stand, I'll pinch off a dozen or so "pinches" and stick them to the fabric on my left shirt/coat arm. During the day I'll constantly be picking a pinch to let it drift down wind.

By the way, while I think of it, you can also keep track of the wind direction by watching mosquitoes and/or dog pecker gnats. The majority of bugs will normally come in or hover on the downwind side of your face/head.

The yarn is my number two favorite wind detector. My all-time favorites are milkweed pods. Milkweed grows pretty much here, there and everywhere. Most everyone knows what they look like so I won't get into that. After the pods fully mature and dry out, they'll split and deposit millions of seeds into the winds. I'll harvest them in early fall and wrap a rubber-band around the pod to keep the floss/silk intact. I'll store them in a sandwich baggie until I need them. Each pod literally holds hundreds or maybe thousands of seeds that are attached to these little silk/floss "legs". The white, hairy silk will float the seed through the wind currents. Here's why I like them best over the polyester yarn: If you study the flow of a pinch of yarn you'll notice if it drifts into a leaf or twig it will stick to the leaf, stopping there. But if you watch the floss of the silk, instead of sticking to the leaf or twig like the polyester, the longer, hairy "arms" of the milkweed will actually roll over most obstructions, continue on to give you a better, more accurate read on the air currents. Not to mention, the price is right since they're natural and free.

BUCKS MASTURBATING: I bet that subtitle raised some eyebrows! Some of these tidbits may not actually help you get a big buck while you're actively hunting, but nature sure is interesting. Once you're aware of what you're seeing you'll have a great subject to talk about around the fireplace with the boys.

Yes, whitetail bucks masturbate. So do lots of other mammals, i.e., bears, elk; dogs, etc. When I lived in Montana, one year, I jumped a young bull elk out of his bed at midday. After he bailed out, I walked over to see if I could learn anything from studying the bed itself. I sure could! There in the bed, anatomically right where his penis should have been, was about a cup of fresh semen. There was no question in my mind about what it was. Thinking back over the years I remembered watching bull elk bugle right from their beds without standing up. I just never checked the beds before, but I'd just about bet there was semen in those beds as well.

Some male dogs will jump your leg while you're sitting in the rocking chair on the front porch if you're not careful. I killed a big black bear boar one year that got too friendly with me. This was back in the mid- 1980s. I really didn't want to shoot him because I was many miles from the road in western Montana and I was actually elk hunting. All I know is the bruin didn't fear me waving my arms and yelling at him. He aggressively approached me emitting a low, guttural rumble while licking the roof of his palate. He was close enough I could see the green grass stains on his teeth. Then he turned broadside and started with the pelvic gyrations, dry-humping and giving me "that look" in his eyes. As soon as he finished, he turned to me and came closer to about fifteen feet. I sunk an arrow into his chest. Frankly, I don't remember any semen on his belly but I also don't recall looking for it either. He likely brushed it off in his death run through the ferns. To this day I believe his intent was obvious.

A lot of animals don't act "normal" when they are sex driven. I have footage of a young (1.5-2.5-year-old) whitetail buck walking 30 feet behind, trailing a single coyote across a field. Coyotes and deer are normally not friends. I personally believe since this footage was taken during the peak of the whitetail rut, the buck was "horny" and the coyote was a female, whereas he was checking her out. I obviously have no way of

Edited video photo screen frame, I'm not making it up!

proving it but that's my opinion. Boys will be boys!

Now, back to the whitetails. I've personally witnessed it at least four different times and got it on video three of those times. All four occurrences were in early November during the peak of the major rut. All four were bucks traveling alone and all four were at or close to scrapes. Three of the bucks were 1.5- or 2.5-year-old (teenagers), although one was a good 4.5-year-old pushing 160 inches. The procedure was almost identical. They lift their tails and severely hump/flex their back, bringing the pelvis and penis forward. The penis actually is inserted into the little "pocket" formed near the base of the sternum/ribcage on the belly. A few pelvic thrusts and it's over. I'm not sure of the biological function, other than maybe releasing sexual frustration since they are alone and not with a doe.

Remember... you likely heard it here first! So... now this book is rated "R" ... sorry!

I'll try to edit some still frames out of the video footage that best show the procedure for those of you who think I'm making this stuff up.

ROUND BALES: When harvesting an alfalfa or hay field, farmers often set those big round bales in a line alongside the edge of the field. Over the years I've used this trick twice to my advantage. Let me build the scenario. There is a block of timber and brush to the north which was the main bedding area. The alfalfa field was just south of the timber. The farmer placed his big round bales in a straight-line running east/west on the north end of the cut field (south end of the timber.) He placed them so the bales butted up to each other similar to the wheels on a vehicle. There were probably a dozen or fifteen bales total. That line of bales created a blockage that forced deer in the timber to walk around on their way to the field in the evening.

Make sure you get permission from the farmer before you do this. You take the end bale and roll it an entire bale width forward, away from the other dozen bales. This creates a gap between the end bale and the rest of them. Then you place a pop-up blind in that gap. This way your pop-up is one bale in and unnoticed, rather than obviously placed on the end.

These set-ups are almost strictly evening sits. Entering before light in the morning is really difficult without disturbing deer feeding the field. The first time I sat the above scenario was on an afternoon, mild southwest wind. The bucks entered the field from the north with a false sense of a headwind when headed to the field to the south. Make yourself a little peephole on the north side of the blind so you can see what's coming from the timber. But be careful of back-lighting.

That very first time I sat the above scenario was an afternoon/evening hunt. The line of bales created an obstacle the deer had to swing around. I remember the first evening/sit I passed up a total of seven racked bucks, including a couple P&Ys, that all walked nonchalantly by me at under 15 yards. The show impressed me enough that I will remember it for the rest of my life.

READING GLASSES: I'll give my brother Gene credit for this tidbit. As we advance in age almost everyone needs reading glasses. They should automatically give them to us when we turn fifty years old or whatever. It seems the older we get the stronger the lens need to be. Right now, I normally buy 250X power. I only use them when reading or on the computer, etc. For those who have never tried them, if I try to read a newspaper without reading glasses everything appears blurred and out of focus. You put reading glasses on and the printing instantly becomes clear.

Now, in the hunting situation, how many times have I been bent over, or on my knees searching for a tiny speck of blood while trying to follow a faint blood trail? It's the same scenario as reading without the peepers. Get yourself a WEAK pair of reading glasses at the Dollar Store or whatever. As I said, I normally use 250X but I keep a pair of 125X power cheapies in my fanny pack to only be used when tracking deer. They will turn an out-of-focus forest floor into a crystal-clear perfectly sharp picture. A lot of the time you don't even need to bend over or squat, you can just walk along a faint blood trail. Having that extra dollar pair of readers could be the difference between the biggest buck of your life and a bad dream.

MORE GENERALIZATIONS: Winds of over 20 MPH alter deer movement. High winds AND no winds decrease normal deer movement. As with a slightly heavier rain, deer will tend to bed in the open/ weeds so they can see better with less dripping noise and blowing vegetation/movement all around themselves. Again, generally, with high winds in the timber hunt lower on the downwind leeward sides other than in valleys.

The first morning of a weather front coming through is always good. Repeating myself, the morning of the year's first hard frost is always outstanding and will be one of the best hunting days of the year.

Human's days are similar to a deer's night. That's when they usually are bedded. Therefore, our afternoons are similar to a deer's morning and it's time to get up. Thus, our mornings are similar to their evenings and it's time to go to bed.

In my opinion, THE best scrape activity is during a cold front in mid to late October. The bucks are ready but the does are not. And the big boys will be moving.

Regarding breeding scrapes, bucks tend to scent check scrapes more in the mornings but actively re-work the scrapes in the afternoons.

Generally, morning hunting conditions are usually poor until mid-October unless a front is coming in.

Hunting afternoons the two or three days before a full moon are generally good.

Two or three days after a full moon you'll generally see a shift to better morning movement.

Every year October 28th through November 4th are generally my favorite days for major daytime mature buck activity in the mid-west and north.

A full moon in mid-November generally has better mid-day activity.

Mid-December generally has good early afternoon movement.

When standing soybeans turn green to brown deer will generally switch to green growth fields/ plots.

After the first two-inch snowfall of the year deer will switch from grazing to browsing and hit weed/ CRP growth. You can prove this to yourself by walking an old logging road the morning after that first 2" snowfall to see all the tracks working the weeds beside the skid roads.

In warmer fall weather they generally prefer green growth, whereas in colder weather they generally prefer standing corn, beans, turnips or sugar beets.

In late December deer will "yard up", even on bare ground, near the best available late season food sources. And they will not hesitate to travel longer distances to those preferred food sources from a better security cover if needed.

After the secondary rut in mid-late December most bucks will again "bachelor up" in groups of the same approximate size/age. But older, big bucks may segregate themselves from the rest of the herd as loners until they shed their antlers.

CHAPTER IX
OBSERVATIONS

Please bear in mind I am not a biologist. But also, please consider my opinions and/or theories that have been formed after many intense decades of trial and error in the field. I'm talking about the practical application of experiences through my own personal observations in the real world, rather than book learned. And I want to share those opinions at least for you to take into consideration.

If you witness something once, it's an occurrence; watching the same thing happen a second time is a possibility; watching a third time is a probability; and a fourth time is highly likely a pattern. As I've previously preached, we all need to slow down and think about what we are seeing in order to truly learn. Recognizing patterns, coupled with our God given ability to reason things out, balances the scales when we are dealing with hunting prey whose senses are so much superior to ours as humans. Patterns are something a wise hunter can take advantage of.

A lot of these opinions are just my own personal impressions. There may have been some instances where you had to be there to agree. And some of these things I am about to mention to you, the readers, you may already know. But a very large percentage have not been lucky enough to witness what I have seen with the conclusions I have formed. Even if you disagree with me, fine, but please take my views/thoughts into consideration.

For decades, the armchair experts have told us coyotes (and

wolves) will routinely concentrate their killing efforts on the young, weak and/or sickly prey. Bull! I'm here to tell you coyotes kill more big, fully mature trophy bucks than all the rest of the deer herd put together. And I'll tell you why. Coyotes are similar to wolves in that they tend to often hunt in packs. And they are VERY efficient killers. I'll mention something here that most readers might not believe but I've witnessed it on three separate occasions. I've seen enough to convince myself a group of coyotes will orchestrate a planned, strategic, deer-drive, purposely working together in a team effort towards a specific intended goal of moving deer into a position to be ambushed.

The first time I witnessed this I was bowhunting alone in northwest Montana, I was overlooking a shallow valley of second growth that had been logged just a couple of years prior. The floor of the valley was not perfectly flat and there were small hilly knobs scattered here and there. Movement caught my eye and I saw a mature whitetail doe and her single fawn feeding a hundred yards below me. More movement from behind them revealed two coyotes hunkered down but sneaking up on the unsuspecting doe and fawn. When they got to maybe 25 yards of the feeding deer, they charged them. The doe cut off to the side, quartering away and I watched in amazement as the one coyote absolutely tried to swing wide in order to push the deer in another direction. It did not work because the deer had a little lead on them. Now comes the interesting part. Suddenly, the original two coyotes joined up with two others. Then it struck me, the first two were "drivers" and the other two singles were each lying in wait on the sides of two little knobs right where the first two were trying to push them to. It was an absolute, planned-out strategic deer drive.

I also found it interesting that after the deer maneuver failed, all four coyotes grouped up and I swear it looked like they were celebrating an "almost" win. All four were jumping around playfully, like they were wagging their tails and yipping as if to say, "Oh man... we almost got 'em... that was fun." I also found it interesting the coyotes never made a noise barking or yipping during the charge, ambush or chase. But as soon as the chase was obviously over, and they grouped up, they started yipping almost like it was part of the ritual/routine. Do not misinterpret the above to translate like they were "cute." They are cold-blooded, heartless killers.

Back to my original statement that coyotes kill more big, mature bucks than all the rest of the deer herd put together, as I previously talked about, full mature whitetail bucks are different. They are like a sub-specie when compared to the rest of the herd. Age demands respect. How many times have we watched a group of deer comprised of does, fawns, yearlings and immature bucks all feeding leisurely in an alfalfa field? If you watch, you will notice they tend to feed as a structured group. This is for security purposes. Always someone looking different directions. More eyes, ears, noses, with safety in numbers.

But then, just at prime time, suddenly, the entire herd looks in the same direction. Here he comes... The Man! He steps into the field, and they all show their respect. In fact, often the herd will systematically adjust their feeding pattern accordingly, offering the best, prime area of the field to the boss-man.

The big, mature buck demands that respect, and he expects it. Therein lies the problem. When a pack of coyotes enter a field of feeding deer, the entire deer herd usually runs away as fast as they can. Basically, this is what saves them. Unlike the rest of the herd, the big mature buck expects and demands respect. He will look at the coyotes and think to himself, "I'm bigger than you... I'm bigger than all six of you put together... I'll take you on!" Unfortunately, what he fails to calculate into the fight is their numbers. Yes, he may weigh more than the whole pack put together, but there might be a half dozen of them or whatever. As big and powerful as that giant buck is, he rarely stands a chance. A couple coyotes will harass his face demanding attention, but meanwhile one or two others will circle and come in from behind. They will hamstring him and rip the femoral artery open. Once that's done, the biggest buck in the world will be dead in a minute and a half. Done deal. If he had only run like the rest of the herd, he likely would have been fine. But, again, this is just another example of how a big buck differs from others in the herd both physically and mentally.

Maintaining the subject of deer as a prey species, let's talk about how cats differ from the canines. In the U.S. we are mostly talking bobcats and mountain lion/ cougars. When a bobcat or cougar is still immature it does not have the jaw strength to break/snap the neck cleanly. Therefore, they will normally go for the throat of its prey, usually a rabbit or squirrel, lock on and hold on tight until the prey passes out and dies. Even when a full mature big tom bobcat gains some weight and strength, I question whether they have enough jaw strength to cleanly break the neck of even a yearling whitetail. Maybe a fawn... as I said, I really don't know, but I tend to think most bobcats will still go for the throat and choke out most deer sized prey as well.

Mountain lions/ cougars are similar but different than bobcats. When they are young, they tend to kill their prey just like a bobcat, by going for the throat and choking or ripping the carotid out. But when they reach full maturity, they gain enough weight and strength to easily snap the necks of their prey. Even an elk sized animal is usually no problem.

It's interesting how they accomplish this. The prey will usually be running, trying to escape. The cougar will "climb on" the side of the deer/elk near where their neck and shoulder meet. Now picture this... he'll hold on with his front legs/claws and then swing the rear portion of his body forward, similar to a pole vaulter, landing half the total body weight of the cougar onto the face and muzzle of the deer or elk. His body weight will force the prey's neck and head into flexion, therefore exposing the back of the neck to a single, powerful bite that snaps the spine/cord and drops the prey instantly, dead in its tracks. Done deal. It's a clean kill with supposedly minimal risk for injury to the predator. Personally, I can agree with this if the prey is a female (doe, cow or calf). But I can see where the prey being an antlered male might create a risk for injury. But the experts tell me not so.

Another thing people often tend not to realize is the fact each specific animal will have a distinct, unique personality... just like humans. In the animal world I use the analogy of dogs. One dog may be really friendly, running up to you wagging his tail and licking you, but the next one will growl and/or bite you. As a sidenote, I have noticed dog personalities tend to coincide with the personalities of their masters. In example, dogs who are family pets with kind, loving masters usually tend to be friendly. Whereas dogs who are beaten and/or abused might tend to bite you more often. Remember this rule if you happen to knock on someone's door to ask for hunting permission. If the yard dog tries to bite you, you'll likely not get permission from that landowner.

There are lovers and fighters in the buck world. The size of their racks or body structures do not seem to matter. I've seen big bodied, fully mature, giant bucks that are timid. In the same respect I've seen medium-sized bucks that are overly aggressive, almost displaying the Napolean complex. I have also noted the body weight of the contenders trumps the rack size. Displaying a big rack might at times intimidate the contender, but a heavier body weight more so intimidates the opposition in my opinion. I've seen it happen enough where I've formed the opinion the sight of a big heavyweight may be enough to win the fight before it even starts. It's been my opinion a giant, truly heavyweight buck with only a small to medium sized rack will usually beat the tar out of a decent sized buck with a giant rack. In a similar respect, a rack with heavier mass will usually whip a long-tined "pretty boy" every time.

Yet another sidenote, I don't want to get into genders here but I'm also of the opinion there are bucks who appear more feminine. I distinctly recall a couple nice sized trophy bucks over the years that didn't reflect the image of a normal whitetail buck in the peak of the rut when masculinity usually seeps from every pore. They had "pretty boy" faces; none of the thick-necked appearances of stud bulls in the rut; more of a sleek body/ physique; and lily-white tarsal glands indicative of no rub-urination when the insides of his hind-legs/hocks should be stained black. They will even stand off to the side and allow an immature, much smaller buck run hot does all around him with indifference. And no, I am not talking a doe with antlers.

Speaking of that, over the years I've seen several what I believe were antlered does. In fact, both my brother and I have bow-killed antlered does in the past. Mine was a full grown "doe." When I walked up to her, I noticed she had been lactating, but she had inch long, hard antlered spikes. I thought she was a doe when I killed her.

In the 2019 and 2020 seasons I had what I believe was another antlered doe walk by me. He/she had a smallish 4x4 (8 point) rack that appeared normal in all respects other than it was in velvet. The antlers also appeared identical in both the 2019 and 2020 making me believe they never hardened and he/she never shed them that winter. Her physique also indicated she wasn't "masculine." She had that pretty face, skinny neck and lily-white hock glands even during the rut. Twice I saw her traveling with two adult does and two yearlings. But she/he showed absolutely no interest sexually the entire month of November.

As an added note of interest, as a kid, in the mid-1960s, while living in Vermont, I killed a fork horn buck on Thanksgiving morning that was in full velvet. Not only was it in velvet, but the small antlers were soft and spongy. But interestingly he did have what appeared to be normal testicles, yet there did not appear to be any injury as is sometimes the case with velvet antlered bucks. I assumed it was some sort of hormonal imbalance.

Back to the subject of specific deer personalities, I believe some bucks tend to be "home bodies" and others tend to wander more during the rut. I'm of the opinion some bucks never or almost never, leave their core area. Or at the very most wander for a day or two and come back home. On the other hand, I have seen bucks with very recognizable antler characteristics (so I would be sure it was the same animal) suddenly disappear and show up a solid five miles away from his primary core area. And, to add even more mystery to the puzzle, he may stray to new turf for upwards of a month or more.

The giant non-typical buck my brother Gene killed in 2004 was a prime example. We nick-named him Woody. Because he ended up measuring in the mid 230-inch category and we hunted him for multiple seasons, he was very recognizable. Old Woody was quite visible in his core area but always seemed to disappear for a MONTH during the rut. I was of the opinion he was one of those bucks that left his preferred core area to breed elsewhere. There are a lot of unanswered questions regarding these buck wandering theories. In essence, apparently not all bucks wander. It's been suggested maybe only half have more than one core area. There are theories that maybe only a year or so after birth they are booted from their birth area by their mothers to establish new turf in order to minimize future inbreeding. Conversely, there are theories they remain in their birth areas the majority of their lives... OTHER THAN the basic month of November when they journey off to establish a secondary core area in order to again minimize inbreeding.

As I stated, there are a lot of unanswered questions we, as students of the whitetails, do not have the answers to yet. These mysteries are one of the major reasons whitetail deer are so well loved.

I waited to track this buck for five hours only to find the coyotes had already gotten him

I wanted to wreck this, but it for five hours only to find

CHAPTER X
LOCATION....... LOCATION......

When I kick the bucket, I think I want to be cremated. It's not that I'm against being buried whole as much as it's being confined to one spot for so long. I want my ashes spread throughout the timber around some of my best deer stands.

Over my many decades of hunting there have been a handful of favorite stands. Each one not only brings back special memories, but each one seems to have its own personality. Usually, they were each special because of some specific characteristic. The reasoning behind the effectiveness of each location is often hard to place a finger on. But the truth is most great stands are great because of some logic we often overlook. Deeper thinking will usually prove it's a security factor, being able to maintain at least some security between point A and point B. It often comes down to logic but sometimes is just a "feeling." i.e., location... location.

Physiologically the stand has good entrance/exit; acceptable cover, yet a decent view in order to study incoming movement; good sun position for lack of morning/evening squinting; comfort and most importantly dependable winds/thermals. Psychologically, all the above equal a feeling of confidence. I probably should also stress right here if you make your stand TOO comfortable you will often have a hard time staying awake. Make sure you're belted in.

I also tend to name my stands just to give them more character. The stand I killed my very first buck was called "the Tater-Hoe." Just for interest-sake, he was a little different. His right antler was a normal 4 points but his left antler grew upwards a couple inches into a club-like blunt spike. At the base of that same spike protruded a downward pointing fork that grew past his left eye and along his face. So, I guess you'd call him a 4x3. I was teased about the fact I told everyone my first buck was a "non-typical." The stand name was derived years prior when my Dad found an old potato hoe that someone carried up into the timber for some unknown reason. Dad killed a big 4x4 from the same stand the year before I got mine. I remember him saying his buck came up the rear of a string of 23 does walking single file past the Tater Hoe.

Another one of my old-time favorite stands did not have a specific name. It was one of those that wasn't a great tree but it was in the right location. I found it after sitting multiple other trees in the area and continuing seeing bucks... big bucks walk by this particular tree. When I was a kid, I remember saying, "in any one area there is one single tree by which more big bucks walk by than any other... and our job was to find that tree and hunt it under prime conditions as often as we can." Yes... I think this was that tree.

The stand was located a couple hundred yards from the Missouri River in eastern Montana. It was in a rectangular block of timber that probably wasn't more than 20 acres or so. More scrutiny revealed just inside the edged tree line was a 20-yard-wide sandy swath that afforded the deer clean, quiet walking with a clear view into the second growth before they emerged into the crop fields to the west for feeding. It really wasn't as much of a grown-up road as it was more of a dried tributary/creek bed that was formed when flood waters of the main river overflowed their banks in occasional years.

The important fact remained that any trails entering the

swath would all filter past this one tree... my tree. Years of sitting the stand taught me a few things. First, I noticed I rarely sat the stand when I didn't see double figures of bucks. If undisturbed, I usually saw ten or twelve bucks per evening. It was obviously more an evening stand than a morning or rut stand. I noticed the stand was much better in the early bow season when the foliage was heavy than after the leaves dropped. This was because the undergrowth was thick enough to see through earlier but still afforded them enough cover in their movement patterns until after the first frosts.

Once the foliage dropped, the older deer, both bucks and does, would shift their movement just fifty yards or so deeper into the timber and bypass the swath. I found it interesting that more mature deer would shift their pattern into the thicker growth after the leaves fell, but the younger yearlings stuck to the swath itself. I also noticed a much higher percentage of deer I saw from that tree were bucks than does. It couldn't be hunted on a west or north wind. But if you had an east or south wind, it was dynamite!

Another interesting fact. This stand was several hundred miles from my home. When I sat the stand for the first time each year, I'd see double figures of bucks. Let's say a dozen for example. Even though I'd hunt elsewhere between sits, the second sit several days later would "only" offer 9 or 10 buck sightings. A few more days off and the third sit I'd only see maybe a half dozen bucks. Even smart hunting and minimal pressure reduced their numbers 50%. I firmly believe, as I've preached for years, one of our biggest advantageous secrets is hunt undisturbed deer.

Buck from the "Beat to Death" stand

I know for a fact I've seen at least two different Boone and

Location... Location...

Crockett bucks from that stand. I know they were both Boone because my hunting partner killed the smaller of the two and he measured 213" net non-typical. And the second one was bigger!

One of my all-time favorite stands was nicknamed the "Beat to Death" stand because of the fact I'd sit the same stand each and every chance I could. I "beat it to death." I don't know why but it was like you couldn't wear it out... they just kept coming. Read on and you tell me if you wouldn't also beat it to death?

This is extremely rare for me, but because of circumstances one year, back in the mid-80s, I sat that same stand three evenings in a row. The first evening I had eight racked bucks slowly walk by me within bow range during the last two hours of legal shooting light. The second evening, what appeared to be eight different racked bucks filed past me... that makes sixteen. The third evening and remember this is the third evening in a row, seven more bucks paraded past me. Although several of them almost had to be repeats, I didn't recognize any of them as bucks I'd seen previously. I recall one was a spike and one was a fork horn but the rest were formed racks of various sizes and styles. The biggest one was a clean 5x5 that would have measured in the low 160s but I didn't have a clean shot.

Taking into consideration likely repeats, that meant still close to 20 some-odd bucks that came within bow range of that single treestand in three consecutive evenings. That's a good stand... heck... that's a great stand! You'd beat it to death too.

You almost had to see the place to understand why I picked it and why it was so good. I haven't even been there for thirty-plus years. It's changed hands a couple times that I know of. I'd bet a lot of money the present owners don't even have a stand near it. It's something that someone needs to point out to you to clearly understand what's going on. When you are elevated in a nearby tree it becomes a little more apparent what's going on. But unless someone actually erects an observation stand to learn from, I doubt if they'd see the reasoning. There are three distinct variations in the undergrowth. Off to the east the timber is extremely open. Just a little off to the east the more mature timber is about the same, but the understory is twice as dense. To the west are thick softwoods. The stand faces north. The softwoods run slightly north/northeast and south/southwest. One needs to be elevated to see the three variations of undergrowth dictating the buck movement.

What happens is the deer travel the edge of the thicker softwoods just one jump away from the safety of the thick cover. The undergrowth edge they walk affords them bodily cover and still their heads protrude above the brush-line where they are able to see out a hundred yards into the open timber. They are able to scent-check variable wind directions and use their vision to check what they can't smell. As I've said before, they see what they can't smell and smell what they can't see. This is a standard way of life for them.

Sometimes great stands are so obvious you overlook them. I hunted one farm for ten years. Ten years is a long time and you'd think you'd get to know the place. It was probably my own fault because the place was a couple hundred miles from home. I got permission just like most people by knocking on the door. I used to drive in along a brushy river bottom. Between the roadway and the river was only about 25 yards but the cover was thick enough that you couldn't see the water unless you walked over to it. When the farmer first took me for a ride around the area he said, "Here's where I park." I never gave it a second thought because the main timber was across a field bordering the river bottom brush. For ten years I just parked where he had, walked across and down the field and around to the timber. We tend to get into ruts. Ten years went by and I never gave a second thought to the situation. Then, one day on my way in I jumped a buck that started to head towards my hunting partner's stand, but then cut out across the field and entered the brush bordering the river. I kneeled down and cupped my ears to listen for the buck crossing the partially frozen river. When I didn't hear any noise of him crossing, I figured he was just standing on the edge watching me. So, I did an about-face and walked back, crossed the field and went through the brush to the river's edge in hopes of bumping him back into the timber and past my hunting buddy.

As I recall it was maybe November sixth or eighth. When I cut through the brush that I'd walked by for ten years I about died. All of a sudden, the river angled abruptly to the left. What for ten years I thought was only 25 yards wide, suddenly turned into a little sanctuary close to 200 yards wide.

As I slipped through the cover, deer got up everywhere. I could hear some of them crossing the river but some of them broke out across the field and past my partner's stand. He said he counted eighteen deer in one bunch including several nice bucks that came across the field from where I'd jumped them. That didn't count what swam the river, those who cut back on me, nor those that puckered up and held tight with their chins on the ground.

Halfway through the thicket I came across some of the hottest rutting sign I'd ever seen. From one spot I could count close to a dozen scrapes, one of which was the size of a small car. Trees were rubbed, brush torn to shreds and mangled branches overhung the scrapes. Half the deer in the county were hanging in that little strip having an orgy while I walked right past them for ten years.

Another of my old favorite stands I used to call "The Black Patch." It's halfway up the side of a mountain of mature timber in northwest Montana a little over a hundred miles from my then home. The shelf is basically open timber but was partially logged off many years ago. What used to be sort of a skid trail cuts just east of the black patch. The trail is almost completely grown in with second growth fir. The Black Patch itself consists of maybe an acre of black pecker-poles with a dozen or so mature lodgepole scattered throughout. The most important part, on the south side of the patch laying on the ground running east/west is the remains of what was a towering Ponderosa pine that measured seven or eight feet across the base. The downed snag lays at an angle that directs the deer under my nearby stand. This is strictly an evening stand. Later in the afternoons deer will move down the mountain to feed and water. Earlier in the day the bucks tend to linger on the shelf waiting for the changing thermals. Additionally, they also tend to cruise the shelf during the rut checking on does. Whether cruising or in hot pursuit of a doe the bucks tend to funnel along the big dead yellow pine and right past my tree.

In the first six years I hunted the stand I've seen two different potential Boone and Crockett non-typical bucks pass under my stand. Unfortunately, once I was in another stand 80 yards away and the other time it was after season scouting. To give you an idea of my persistence, consider the fact I lived over a hundred miles one-way from the stand. It was the late season in Montana. Monday through Friday for a week straight I cut out of my office early, drove 100 miles, slipped unheard into the stand with my bow, knowing he might hang up on the shelf or pass by with a doe just before dark. I got in less than a half-hour of prime time before dark. Then, I'd drive another 100 miles home. I did that five-weekdays in a row, plus a two-day weekend at each end, so a total of nine days straight trying to kill him. I saw him twice but not in bow range. Unbeknownst to me, I later found out he was poached that last week of season when a local bragged he popped him under the light one night on the way home from the bar. He supposedly had seventeen total points including a drop-tine and measured 198 inches non-typical. I hope the maggot is proud of himself.

Another one of my old favorite stands lays right smack dab in the center of a jungle of river bottom tangles. Basically, it's a rectangular patch, but the secret lies in what's left of an old fence that bisects the patch diagonally. Time has taken its toll on the old fence and only two strands of wire remain. The undergrowth in the area consists of vines and briars that have overgrown the two strands forming a virtual impenetrable wall of debris. Halfway through the patch there is one... and only one, break in the wire strands. Every deer trail in the entire area funnels through that one break in the old wire strands. Actually, I found the spot when I was blood trailing a buck on the edge of the patch. He went through the break and did a figure "8" back through it again before I finished him. I thought it was rather strange and a little investigation afterwards showed it was basically the only place he could cross without great difficulty. Low and behold, a perfect tree sits just fifteen yards to either side of the crossing.

These downed/fallen trees; old broken fence line/wires and different understory densities are things we can't see from aerial photos and/or topographical maps. These are the minute pieces of the puzzle we need to see for ourselves with boots on the ground while walking around slowly and THINKING about what you are seeing. Sometimes I feel like God puts these set-ups out there purposely and it's our job to find them. Once we do find them, He smiles and rewards us with big bucks year after year.

This buck's figure 8 lead to the perfect tree

CHAPTER XI
BREAKING TABOO

Let's talk deer beds; not actually the beds themselves as much as the areas of bedding... the deer's bedroom, so to speak.

Over the years we seem to have been programmed to follow a set of rules in life. Rules of acceptance. Deer hunting isn't any different. One of the standard unbroken rules is: never hunt bedding areas because you will disturb the deer and they will be harder to hunt. I guess that is true in a sense, but I sometimes disagree as there are, as in most situations, variables.

One of the reasons people say you can't hunt bedding areas is because the deer will be immobile and the hunter mobile. Therefore, he will detect you long before you detect him. There is almost no question about that outcome. They choose their bedding sites for security reasons, and if chosen well they will be almost impossible to approach undetected. That's the very basis behind their locations. I use the analogy of locking yourself in your own motel room (bedroom) when sleeping in a bad neighborhood.

If you were locked in your room and someone tried to enter, it would be almost impossible for them to break the lock and enter without you being awakened to detect their approach.

But if someone were to be lurking in the shadows of the closet inside the room before you arrived, you would become a much more vulnerable target.

This is how I hunt bedding areas. Don't get me wrong, the

conditions have to be just right. But it can definitely be done. The secret is to have the situation already set up and in place; the stand already hung; the scent dissipated; the weather and wind conditions being perfect and consistent before you even consider it. The problem is all those factors don't often come up. But being aware of their possibilities is money in the bank.

A good treestand location is imperative. You'll usually not be able to pull off this technique except from an elevated position because of scent. You'll want a stand with plenty of background cover around you... a dark closet for you to leap out of, so to speak.

Hunting deer movement patterns involves catching the deer going to and from feeding and bedding areas. This usually entails a pattern of movement at just certain hours, therefore the hunter only has to stay in position for a few hours at a time. This is not so when hunting bedding hours. The entire philosophy behind hunting in the bedding area is to get there before the deer arrives, stay there all day long undetected and leave only after all the deer have moved out to feed.

It can be done, but then again, a hunter has to go prepared both physically and psychologically. This involves a great deal more than just sitting a morning or evening stand. You must adapt, and I must say it usually takes a certain type of individual to pull it off.

Make sure you have a good comfortable stand you can relax in. Standing with one foot on a limb isn't going to get it. Have a stand with a seat so you can stand and/or sit to vary your physical position without getting cramped up. Also, as ALWAYS, make sure you wear a safety belt/harness because you will be getting sleepy and very likely might doze off.

It's okay to urinate from the stand but having to move off for a bowel movement will ruin your day. Speaking of this, it's not a good idea to fast during a hunt. It might be okay to fast the day before to keep your bowels empty, but make sure you eat a good, stick to the ribs breakfast before you get on stand or you'll freeze out. Trust me, this is no lie. I tried it once. Many years ago, in my youth I missed an easy shot at a deer I should have killed. So, in my immature thinking I decided to punish myself by not eating again until I bagged one. Yeah, I know, I'm an idiot. The second morning on stand, after not eating at all the day before, was really gruesome. It was only in the upper twenty-degree range, just below freezing temperatures and I couldn't stand it. I'd lived in northwest Montana and Vermont so I was used to the colder temperatures, but that morning with no food in me and the temperature at only 30 degrees was one of the coldest I've ever encountered. My core temperature was freezing. With no food in your stomach your body isn't generating its own heat and you'll freeze out. I've been colder hunting on an empty stomach at 20 degrees above zero, than hunting on a full stomach at 20 degrees below zero.

Getting back to the situation above, I luckily shot a deer that afternoon so I didn't have to torture myself the next morning. People say a person hunts better on an empty stomach but I don't know if I agree. Standard Wensel rule: don't ever go grocery shopping or stand hunting all day on an empty tank. Anyway, have yourself a good hearty breakfast if you're planning to sit all day. Make your wife get up really early and make you fresh coffee, bacon, eggs, hash browns, biscuits, etc. She can go back to bed after you leave. Okay.. maybe I did get a little carried away there.

For food I take in plenty of low odor/high energy stuff.

Sandwiches work well. Take a couple extra and eat one every few hours so it will both keep you awake and break up long hours of inactivity. Or eat only a half a sandwich at a time.

You might also want to consider a thermos of hot soup on stand. That works wonders both mentally and physically. Another good idea is to take a wide-mouth thermos packed with four or five pre-boiled wieners and fill the tank with boiling broth, soup or whatever. Then in a separate baggie keep yourself a couple "mustard/ketchup sandwiches." When it comes time remove a couple wieners and roll them in a mustard covered slice of bread... presto.. A steamy hot, gut-warming hotdog fifteen feet up in a tree.

I also suggest taking at least one extra drink more than you expect. I always go for the bottles with the screw cap lids. First off, it'll make a lot less noise than opening a can of whatever. Secondly, you can take a swig or two of drink and replace the screwcap rather than being forced to drink it all at once because the can is open.

I guess I'm a muncher. I prefer food I can munch on all day rather than eating it all at once. For example, I prefer M&M Peanuts; chocolate covered raisins or walnuts, or chocolate covered coffee beans, rather than one whole candy bar consumed in fifteen seconds flat. By the way, those chocolate covered coffee beans will help keep you awake with the hit of caffeine. Another great snack for all-day sits is a bag of pistachio nuts where you have to open each nut one at a time.

Another great snack is dehydrated fruit and/or jerky. It's lightweight, usually has a low odor and tends to swell inside your stomach when you have a drink with it. So, it keeps you feeling full. But realize there's a big difference between having a full belly and full intestines. I think I've made my point.

Enter the stand prepared to endure the elements and stay all day if needed. I try to enter the stand at least an hour before the very first hint of "pink light." Yes.. you have to sit there in the dark for that first hour... sorry.

If you jump deer in the dark while entering the stand from the back door, you're already late and will need to come earlier in the future.

Always remember the first deer to enter the bedding grounds will often be the bucks, so it's of the utmost importance they are not disturbed. The same is true for the evening departure. Because you have been there all day you may have the desire to get down a little earlier. Just remember the last ones to move will likely be the studs. Don't let the anxiety of leaving early ruin your 12-hour efforts.

I usually either wear wool or fleece type of materials at that time of year. One reason is warmth but the other is silence. Because we are dealing with such a close-range situation, noises which you would otherwise not take time to consider might very well be of utmost importance. I might hunt five or six different farms every year. A lot of trees where I hunt vary but are often the shaggy-barked varieties. Because of the fact I have a wool or fleece jacket on my back, any movement against the trees causes some low-volume noise. Sometimes I feel like my back/coat is a piece of Velcro against the tree when I shift just slightly to take the shot. I know it doesn't sound like much to us, but believe me, that slight noise can completely ruin an otherwise perfect situation.

My solution is to carry an extra garment to wrap around the

tree. I use an old long-sleeve camouflage T-Shirt and tie the arms together around the tree trunk and lean my back against the cotton of the shirt rather than the tree bark. Try it... perfect silence.

Another item you may want to consider on an all-day sit in cold temps is an old wool blanket.

You can usually pick up those olive-drab green or gray wool military blankets at Army/Navy Surplus stores or on the internet. Consider both wool and/or polar fleece blankets. The wool ones are heavier and therefore warmer. And if it's good quality wool, it will maintain the natural lanolin content. In fact, it's unbelievable how waterproof a good wool blanket is. The polar fleece "throws" are not as warm but much lighter weight and inexpensive.

Roll them up and stuff one in your backpack. If you don't need it for warmth you can use it as a cushion in your treestand. But when it gets bitter cold you can wrap the blanket around your shoulders like a little teepee "tent". You won't believe how much warmer you'll be with that layer of body-warmed air trapped between you and the blanket. And when a potential shot should present itself you can just let the blanket/wrap fall back off your shoulders against your tree.

Individuals vary. Some prefer to hold their weapon in their hands. I prefer to hang it close by on a hook. I find not having to hold it all day tends to make me sit still with less movement.

Breaking Taboo

Midday activity can be dramatic

The same seems to apply whether sitting or standing. I tend to not fidget as much when seated. An upright standing human in a tree seems fine for skinny guys. I've found that a standing fat guy seems to appear to be too bulky when upright. I'm more concerned about my movement than I am about my bulk. I might mention here that I have practiced and learned to shoot well from a seated position. Don't get me wrong, I prefer to be standing up for the shot so I can rotate better if needed. But I will not hesitate to shoot from a seated position if I think standing up may get me busted.

Some people don't properly relate to how a deer actually beds. They think he finds a spot, lays down and doesn't move until dark. That could be the case but usually not. More often than not the buck will be up and down throughout the day, shifting his position in response to thermals, doe activity, pecking order, internal and external pressure, etc. The point is they are up and down all day long WITHIN the bedding area. Of course, hardly anyone knows this because we have been programmed to stay out of the bedding areas so as not to disturb them.

Mid-day activity within the bedding grounds can be very dramatic, especially during the rut. You'll find cruising bucks will slip through the bedding grounds in search of a ripening doe. They have been programmed not to expect any disturbances as long as they stay within the confined area. Because of its tight security cover, they will move around freely, being dependent on other bedded animals to warn them of any dangers. This is where our human ability to reason works to our advantage.

You'll find that a great amount of breeding activity that takes place right around the scrape is nighttime activity while we are curled up at home. Whereas a lot of daytime breeding activity takes place within the bedding areas in the middle of the day. Remember, because deer are primarily nocturnal critters their nights are our days and our days are their nights. Think about how many times you've heard of guys sitting scrapes all day long without seeing much, or at least not what they were expecting, only to return the next day to find the scrapes actively and aggressively reworked. Nighttime rutting activity has prevailed here. Now, don't take me wrong, rutting behavior will occur whenever and wherever the situation is right. I'm just trying to make the point that a lot of guys are hunting at the wrong times in the wrong places.

When scouting bedding areas go in with the assumption you are going to be spooking deer, because you will be. This means we should only do this during the off seasons. I much prefer doing this on a day with some snow cover since it's so much easier to read the sign on snow. Accept an educational morsel whenever it's offered, but I find it really hard to scout and think about what you are seeing while you are actually hunting.

There are both advantages and disadvantages to wind velocity when sitting in bedding areas. A calm/still day is great because you can hear deer approaching. A brisk wind makes them nervous. In fact, when it gets too windy they will often leave the "security" of thicker cover and shift their beds into more open, grassy areas where everything isn't moving and they can see better. Sometimes the shifting positions of bedded does will be mistaken for rutting behavior by the nearby bucks and it will initiate a chain reaction of movement within the immediate area so watch for it.

Not enough attention is focused on how or where deer bed down. In a nutshell you'll notice most of the thicker areas will be utilized as bedding grounds because of the security factors. Close investigation will reveal deer prefer to bed on the downwind side of a block of timber. Read that sentence again. And they usually bed with the wind at their backs. This way they are using the density of the terrain as security. At the sametime, they are using their sense of smell, which is their most dependable sense, to protect their most vulnerable backsides.

One of my favorite examples of permanent beds was in a block of timber I used to hunt in Montana. When the rancher first cleared the field on the east side of the timber he bulldozed all the bigger trees into piles on the east side of the block. This area has a very predominant wind coming from the west. Behind, within and under every log pile on that east edge there are very distinct permanent beds, beds that are used so often they are clear of debris right down to the bare dirt.

Think about the security of this situation. The deer can lay there in the cool shade of the logs, out of the wind and yet visually detect any activity in the field in front of them. The steady breeze coming through the timber over their backs protects their blind side. If any disturbance comes across the field to the east they are able to slip undetected upwind (where they can smell is safe) into the density of the thick cover. If any disturbance should come at them from across the field from the north or south they can easily skirt the timber in the opposite direction of the trouble and loop back upwind away from it. It's brilliant. They do these maneuvers every day and we humans usually don't have a clue... it's that simple!

> **"The only thing that is even slightly predictable about big bucks is the way they relate to terrain"**

CHAPTER XII
THE UPS AND DOWNS

I always try to hunt smart, or at least sneaky. The sneakier we are, the less disturbance we make. And the less disturbance we make the more we get to hunt undisturbed deer moving like they are supposed to move. I always tend to go way out of my way in order not to disturb an area, especially on entrance/exit.

So, it was in the early morning hours of October 23, 2011. I wanted to hunt a new stand I'd nick-named "Little Beaver". Its positioning was on a little flat shelf just below the south edge of a tiny "beaver pond." There were no beavers, never were, but we still referred to it as that. With favorable winds coming out of the south and southwest, the ladder's position had my scent drifting across the water's edge at my back. The pond itself wasn't 30 yards in diameter but it did hold water and created some structure involving a pinch between its edge and a dry creek bed fifty yards below it.

Any normal guy would have just followed the dry creek bed in. But I decided to get more unorthodox in hopes of disturbing fewer deer on my entrance. It dictated I follow an old skid road along the top of the mountain, then dropping down a finger ridge into the dry creek bottom and following the creek bed for fifty yards or so before I entered the stand itself. It was quite a way out of my way but it certainly seemed like the intelligent thing to do in order to hunt smart and trick them.

In the pre-dawn darkness, I negotiated my way down the main finger ridge until I was just above the dry creek bed. There was a small, knife-like secondary finger maybe only ten feet wide dropping thirty to fifty feet down into the creek. It had a pretty good deer trail on it because it was the most logical place to cross, but it was steep.

When dropping down any steep incline, if there are small trees/saplings growing on the steep sidehill I'll often turn around, face into the hill, hold onto saplings, dig the toes of my boots in and back slowly down the grade. But this small finger didn't have any saplings. Therefore, my intent was to squat down, sit on the ground, dig the heels of my boots in while I slid my butt downward to the bottom.

I put my flashlight in my mouth, held my bow in my right hand and was in the process of squatting when the edge I was standing on fractured off... Over I went! Don't forget this is pitch dark. I instinctively tried to dig my heels in while still sitting upright which worked only too well. Momentum won out and my upper body weight flipped me head over heels, or maybe more accurately heels overhead twice... two complete flips. Either way, doing two complete front-flips in the dark, in the middle of nowhere down the steep mountain was not good. After my second flip I tumbled to my side and rolled the rest of the way to the bottom. I remember rolling over some 6-8-inch diameter logs laying on the hill side. Each felt like someone hitting me with a baseball bat. Remember, "My name is Cliff... drop over sometime." Finally, I came to a stop at the bottom. For a couple seconds I just laid there thinking to myself, "Golly gee, gosh darn, son of a gun!", or something like that but maybe not in those words. Then I realized I was hurt.

Some of this is unbelievable to me. Before the fall I was wearing my excellent Bison Gear wool backpack with the two arm/shoulder straps and the waist belt buckled. Somehow the whole pack came off and was gone... the entire backpack, gone. The flashlight I had in my mouth also got turned off and was missing. Even though it was dark I located my backpack and crawled over to it knowing I had a second/spare flashlight in the front pocket of the pack. As I crawled to it something poked me in my thigh. Looking down I saw it was the nock end of one of my loose broadheads. Without really thinking, I just brushed it aside and got to my flashlight.

When I turned it on, I suddenly realized how incredibly lucky I was. The nock of the arrow I just poked into my thigh was 50/50 being a broadhead rather than the nock. I'd rolled right over my recurve bow, breaking my beautiful custom rattlesnake skin covered bow quiver. There were five razor-sharp broadheads laying scattered all around me in the dark. I'd rolled right through five potential tragedies being extremely lucky I didn't impale myself.

I was numb and sore, then realized I'd broken a front tooth off but there was no blood, no apparent broken bones and I was able to slowly stand up.

Gathering everything up I placed the broadheads into the hood of the broken quiver and put them into the safety of my backpack and limped the rest of the way into the stand.

An hour later, at first shooting light, I heard something coming. It was only a spikehorn buck, but I thought I should stand up just in case something was following him. When I went to stand up, I realized I couldn't stand. My left leg wasn't working. I ended up pulling myself up by my arms via a handy limb, then thinking maybe I better wrap it up and get out of there.

I had a tough time just climbing down from the ladder stand. My leg apparently seized up from the time I climbed up until the time I came down. I found I could put weight on my leg but couldn't get back up the hill I'd fallen down. So, I limped my way up the dry creek bed a long way until I came to a more gradual incline I knew of. It ended up taking me two hours and twenty minutes to limp out the distance that should have taken me a half hour max.

I think we tend to sometimes rely on technology a little too much. I'm honestly not much into cell phones, but I always carry one for safety and communications if needed. But the reality was there no cell service in the bottoms. My wife was not home, brother Gene was a hundred miles away, likely in another tree stand, and no one really knew where I was but him. When I hunt alone, I always leave a note at home in an obvious place saying what stand I intend to hunt, etc. In the evenings we always call each other, not only to exchange sightings but for safety purposes. We always need to think about the facts such as these scenarios. What if I had broken something before first light in the morning and was stranded helpless? No one would have even known about the injuries until that evening. Then, IF my brother would have come to check it was at least a two-hour drive, not to mention you'd likely be dealing with trauma, bleeding, shock, hypothermia, etc. It's certainly something to think seriously about... we're talking death here.

My injury was strange in that there were luckily no fractures. I took the blunt of the fall on the big muscles in my left thigh. Afterwards it felt like mush. The doctor diagnosed it perfectly and my prognosis was precisely what he predicted. Almost my entire leg turned black and I limped for just over a month. Just for the fun of it I measured some of my bruises I could reach. I had over 180 square inches in one bruise all the way from the top of my hip to my ankle. The doc mentioned people who are on blood thinners may be in even deeper trouble with internal bleeding like that. Being late October and one of my favorite times to hunt, as hard as it was, I forced myself to lay around and heal for a couple days. Afterwards, I just paced myself, allowing more time to walk in and out. Maybe it was meant to be because I killed my target buck (Hurley-190 1/8 inch NT) a week later on November 1st.

I really don't want to preach safety here but I also wanted to touch on a couple other dangerous situations absolutely no one ever thinks about. These are all scenarios I learned myself the hard way that easily could have been fatal.

Dry Rot: Before the season each fall, I try to detail my stands that were left in the timber from previous years. We trim out any shoots that grew; level them, etc. But a lot of guys forget to test the rachet straps because the "look" fine. Five years ago, I changed my mind (thank you Lord) on sitting a morning stand before light when I remembered I'd not detailed it for that season. I came back to sit it another afternoon rather than before light in the morning. On climbing into the ladder, the very first thing I did was snap my safety belt onto the anchor. This particular stand had a 3-inch screwed-in eyelet already in place. I snapped on, turned around and sat down on the flip-down seat. Instantly, two of those three-inch wide heavy-duty nylon straps that hold the seat up broke simultaneously. They looked absolutely perfect but obviously had dry-rotted. Luckily, my safety strap worked perfectly, caught me and saved me from a twelve-foot fall. Be aware of dry rot!

Another we never think about: Brother Gene used to have a hang-on tree stand in a big cottonwood tree behind his home on the Bitterroot River bottoms in Montana. He left it there for years. In order to climb into the stand, he had those screw-in tree steps. Unknown to us, if those screw-in tree steps are left in the tree permanently, after a couple years, the solid wood around the threads of the screw-in part will die and turn basically to sawdust. Your bodyweight will pop the step right out. So, if you have a good stand you want to leave in place for years, always un-screw and re-screw the steps annually, even if you just shift them a couple inches to the side. Gene found this out the hard way and practically gutted himself on the lower screw-in steps on his way down. Luckily, he was only on the third step up.

Another tip to consider when using screw-in tree steps. Back in the 1960s I shot a buck one afternoon. Although it was a lethal shot, he took a couple jumps and just stood there dying. I wanted to get another arrow into him but couldn't so I lowered my bow on the haul-line and quickly started to descend the tree. Where I messed up was when I hung the stand, I clipped off a one-inch limb right near where I placed the screw-in step. Rather than clipping it close to the tree I cut it off maybe six inches out. So, in my hast, I mistook the cut limb as one of my tree steps. It didn't hold and I fell seven or eight feet landing on my back. Out of pure luck the farmer had previously cleared some brush and piled it near the base of my tree, whereas I landed right on top of the brush pile where it cushioned my fall. And yes, I finished the buck.

DVT- Deep Vein Thrombosis: When we humans reach about fifty years old our gluteal muscles (our buttocks) turn to mush. Don't ask me why, but they just do. It's just a medical fact.

That's why they tell us older people not to drive long distances in a car for more than a couple hours without stopping, stretching and/or at least getting out and walking around the vehicle a couple times. Believe it or not, the same thing is true when sitting on the stool for you long time/ marathon bathroom readers.

I'll write more on my DVT occurrence later, but the scary fact is you can actually die from sitting in a tree stand for too long. Without standing up and stretching, the edge of the tree stand seat will cut off the blood supply to your lower extremities. The blood stops flowing and starts to clot. It's very similar to a tourniquet. When the blood clot eventually breaks loose it can be deposited into your lungs and you will die.

One guy tried to convince me that's how General Custer actually died and that's why they refer to it as "Custer's Last Stand." But I ain't buying that one. But I know I've been sitting at this typewriter for five hours now and I'm getting dizzy.

CHAPTER XIII
AHH… CHEW

She says, "Goes in tight."

He says, "What?"

She says, "You just sneezed. 'Goes in tight' is the way of saying 'God Bless you' in German."

He says, "So?"

She says, "So, don't you just love how worldly I am speaking different languages?"

He says, "Whatever. Turn the light off."

Actually, it's spelled "Gesundheit" but is pronounced "goes in tight" with the accent on "in". So, when someone sneezes:

If you're German you say, "Goes in tight."

If you're a Christian you say, "God bless you."

If you're an atheist, or maybe a lazy Christian, you say, "bless you" and foolishly leave the God part out.

If you're a terrorist you say, "decent blast."

If you're a mother you YELL… "COVER YOUR MOUTH WHEN YOU SNEEZE."

We're going to eventually get to the finer points of sneezing and deer hunting, (yes, there is a relationship here). But before that, I want to expand a little on sneezing techniques.

I know guys who loosely clench their fists like they're holding a tube. They sneeze directly into their fist/tube. This very effectively fills your palm with millions of germs. Then, for the next hour or three, everyone you shake hands with or touch gets affected. It's not a healthy habit. Basically, sneezing into your hand has no effect other than maybe something similar to the choke on your shotgun barrel/pattern. I'm saying you want to STOP the spray, not just change the pattern.

Proper sneezing etiquette is to sneeze into a handkerchief, tissue, or your sleeve/forearm opposite your elbow. This keeps the spray minimal and isolated into an area not often touched. If you question the effectiveness of a good sneeze, next time you feel one coming on, position your face about 6 to 8 inches from a mirror and let 'er rip. You'll get my drift (no pun intended). Please pass the Windex.

Now, let's talk about human sneezes. First off, who made up that old wives tale about looking at the sun will cause you to sneeze? I ain't buying it. I've looked at more than my share of sunrises and sunsets and can't ever remember looking at one that made me sneeze.

Onto the finer points of sneezing and hunting. Sneezing is usually caused by an air borne irritant, be it pollen, dust, pepper or whatever. That's why we have nose hairs, to help block out those floating irritants from entering our lungs. Breathing through your mouth doesn't filter irritants as well. There's yet another good reason why never get yourself out of breath.

If you should feel a sneeze coming on when in the timber, the first thing to do is pinch your nostrils with both fingers and "scratch the itch." Rub the outside of your nose. Finger insertion is not necessary and may even be detrimental.

If an external nasal massage does not do the trick and you still feel the blast coming on, all is not lost because Uncle Barry is going to teach you how to sneeze perfectly silently. The negativity of a loud sneeze when hunting is obvious. They say it's impossible to sneeze and keep your eyes open, that it's an involuntary muscle contraction. I don't know but I think I've almost mastered it.

Have you ever seen the slo-mo clip filmed with a little medical camera that shows what happens internally when you sneeze? It's impressive. Every single cell, muscle and organ within your body shakes violently when we sneeze. It's like an internal explosion. This devastating effect is caused by residual air being forced from your lungs. Hence, lies the secret. In the milliseconds just before you sneeze if you forcefully expel all the air from your lungs there is no internal air to discharge. JUST before you sneeze, forcefully exhale, close your mouth and pinch your nose shut. The sneeze will occur but there will be no blast of air because there's almost no air in your lungs. Your body and shoulders will just mildly "jump" in an almost totally silent sneeze. And, with practice, you can keep your eyes from blinking if you desire, so you'll not miss out on anything.

I recall one evening in mid-October a couple years ago when I was perched near a sweet oak dropping acorns constantly. I had five does and yearlings feeding within 20 yards of me. I did the silent sneeze three times and none of the feeding deer even raised their heads. I'm telling you, hunters and our military snipers need to thank Uncle Barry for this great tip. You're welcome! Remember, you read it here first!

In an equally important part of this life changing chapter on sneezing and hunting, I'd like to talk about deer sneezing. There is an absolute difference between a deer snort, a wheeze and a sneeze. The first two are functional within the deer world. The function of a snort is to clear the deer's nasal passages of mucus. I like to tell people it's mucus… but it's snot (get it?) Sorry!

Anyway, the function of the snort is to clear the nasal passages of mucus so they can smell things better. They are blowing out the snot so they can better inhale foreign scent molecules. I'll get into this somewhat later, but a deer has approximately 330 million scent receptors in his nose. By snorting, they are moistening the orifice. A moist/wet orifice can and will pick up scent molecules floating in the air easier. We've all seen an alerted buck licking his nose constantly. There you go, they are licking their noses in order to moisten the orifice to be able to pick up scent molecules better. That's the function of a snort.

The wheeze is sometimes referred to as the "snort-wheeze" making it somewhat confusing. I personally only refer to it as a wheeze. They are totally different in the respect a snort is exhalation and a wheeze is inhalation.

The wheeze is nothing but communication within the deer herd showing dominance to and over subordinate animals within the social herd structure. That's the function of the wheeze and without a doubt my favorite deer calling technique which we'll get into more elsewhere.

The deer sneeze is likely something you've heard or read very little about until now. That's something I find hard to believe because it will make you a better deer hunter. Simply just being aware of it makes it very important. A lot of this info is uncharted waters. Let me say this, three or four years ago I kept track of deer sneezes I heard n the woods that fall. Believe it or not, I heard EIGHT bucks sneezing before I saw them. As I said, knowing what to listen for makes all the difference in the world. A lot of this is theory and strictly my own opinion. I hope it will stimulate the opinions of others who will now pay attention and hand down their thoughts to future generations who will now know what to listen for.

Another factor I've noticed is the sex ratio. Maybe it's totally coincidental, I don't know, but 100% of the deer I've visually verified sneezing have been bucks rather than does. Therefore, what I'm about to tell you doesn't make sense. Bear with me.

I've got two personal theories on deer sneezes. In no special order, almost all deer sneezes (nearly 100%) I've heard were in October or early November. This makes perfect sense for theory number one. Additionally, bear in mind I've lived in Iowa for the last 20+ years (1999). The almost thirty years prior I lived in northwestern Montana. I can't honestly ever remember hearing a deer sneeze in Montana. It's possible I did hear deer sneezing but didn't know what I was hearing or maybe didn't pay any attention to it in my youthful ignorance. The point being neither western Montana nor eastern Montana had any mast crops of hardwood trees. There was next to zero scrounging for acorns in the oak leaves.

Herein lies my first theory. When acorns, beech nuts or any mast crop falls into the dry leaves beneath the "dripline" of each tree, deer have to scrounge for them. Think about it. October is the normal "Indian summer" type of weather.

Cool nights with dry, sunny days and mild breezes. Autumn is here. Along with acorns falling, colorful foliage dries, dies and flutters to the forest floor.

Some oaks produce sweeter acorns than others. I refer to them as "sweet oaks" because they seem to attract deer like a kid to candy. Because multiple deer end up spending many hours walking around in dry leaves under certain trees, the dry leaves get pulverized. You will likely see where I'm going here. If you really look close beneath the drip line of a sweet oak, you'll notice the leaves have been pulverized into a fine dust of leaf particles.

Every day while acorns are falling nature drops a new supply of nuts under each tree until the cache runs out. I believe with the daily scrounging the deer inadvertently inhaled some pulverized leaf dust causing them to sneeze just like us and table pepper. I've personally videotaped a single buck sneezing a couple dozen times within only a couple minutes. Sneezing is the noise you need to hear and pay attention to. We've probably all heard it multiple times for years and just didn't know what it was. Once you've heard it you had better pay attention, stand up and get ready. You'll note it sounds very much like a dog sneezing. But also note it's a completely different sound than a wheeze or a deer snorting.

My second sneeze theory may shock a lot of people. There's an interesting critter called a bot fly. Allegedly, they are our fastest flying insect. Supposedly they've been clocked at 800 MPH... but I ain't buying that either. First off, how'd they clock him? We're talking a fly here. It seems like one flying by at 800 MPH would be tough to keep track of. And seeing 768 MPH is the speed of sound wouldn't they be creating little sonic booms? Whatever.

Anyway, not only can the bot fly haul ass but she can also hover. Now, get ready... the female bot fly hovers close to the head/face of the host specie (the deer) and while hovering ejects her larvae into the nostrils of the deer (a feat that is nothing to sneeze at... no pun intended... sorry... I couldn't help myself)! The ejected larvae then migrate into the retropharyngeal cavity at the internal base of the deer's tongue where they develop. They grow into large grubs, sometimes over an inch long, in a cluster of 20 or so. After they mature, they again begin to migrate within the nasal passages. The sneezing indicates the migration of mature larvae. They simply "tickle" the deer inside the nasal cavities, whereas health issues to the host animals are relatively unwarranted. I know this stuff may be hard to swallow (no pun intended) but ask your local taxidermist if he's ever encountered bot fly larvae while sawing a skull for a European mount? Or if he's ever found bot fly larvae laying on the floor the following day after hanging a buck carcass head-down overnight to cool?

So, there you have it. Learn to listen for deer sneezes. When you hear one you had better get ready. And, if he's a shooter, here's hoping your arrow "goes in tight" right behind the shoulder (sorry... I couldn't help myself again).

CHAPTER XIV
PONDERING

I question whether age or experience tends to make us think more philosophically. Maybe it's a combination of both. I know I've been thinking a lot recently about my many decades as an avid whitetail hunter. Maybe it's because at this late age in life I know the sun is setting. I've concluded I've truly been blessed with my entire life, and I'm so thankful for it. I've said this before, I don't know of very many people who can say if they needed to restart life again they wouldn't change much.

Regardless of whether your hunting techniques mirror those of a canine, feline or raptor, we are basically all predators. In a nutshell, for those who have never contemplated it, human hunters who track down their game like the familiar deer trackers of our northeastern U.S., or even those who hunt via organized deer drives in aggressive pursuit (yes, I've three times witnessed coyotes orchestrate a purposeful deer drive), these hunters pursue game similar to canines. It's their aggressive, come from behind and overpower, offensive maneuvers, similar to an offensive, rather than defensive, football team.

Hunters who still-hunt, those who silently stalk their prey, are mostly like felines. In fact, felines are the epitome of stalkers. Whereas, hunters who silently sit on stand, be it perched in a tree stand or maybe a ground blind, are most like raptors, our birds of prey. It's interesting to think about hunters who are a combination of each method. You may have a hunter who is sitting on stand (raptor) who has a deer slip by him out of range. Because there's a fresh snow, he leaves his stand and begins tracking the game (canine). Then, he notices the game is starting to feed, so he slows down and starts sneaking/stalking (feline). Interesting that we as humans have the option of which way we pursue on any one day. Just for arguments sake, big bucks can and are killed using all three methods of pursuit, but it's my opinion most fully mature animals usually have superior senses to humans, so we are usually better off staying immobile, like a raptor, and letting the game make the move. That's just my opinion but in the same respect I enjoy being a canine, feline and/or a raptor.

Regardless of whether your hunting techniques mirror those of a canine, feline or raptor, we're basically all carnivorous predators. I'm big on analogies and got to thinking how each of our hunting strategies and/or philosophies relate to sports.

As youngsters, we all have the opportunity to participate. We usually favor the sport or recreational activity we tend to be best at. We have team sports and we have individual athletes. Frankly, most team sports are dated. I genuinely feel sorry for kids who LOVE team sports. There's absolutely nothing wrong with them but it's somewhat depressing to know you have to give up certain sport activities when we are still relatively young. Because of physical limitations and changes, most people can't continue to participate as an athlete in many of the physical sports.

Just using round figures, say our lifespan is 80 years old. A kid that LOVES football usually goes from sandlot ball; to high school; to college, and if they are really outstanding (love for the sport aside), they may even play in the NFL. But the cold hard fact remains by the time they are forty (and often much sooner) they are done as an active participant. How would we like it if our love of hunting suddenly came to an end when we turned 35 or 40, forcing us to only watch hunting on TV, reading about it, or maybe being the camp cook? My point is, we as hunters are so fortunate and unique in the respect that as long as we can get around, we can still participate. Sure, we can't tear up the mountains like we could in our youthful prime. We have to adapt, slow down, apply using our heads more so than our physical brawn. But the fact is by adapting, we can still remain in the game as more than just spectators. We may have to slow our pace; hunt with a "walking stick" (never call it a cane); maybe limit ourselves to ground blinds and/or still hunting/stalking rather than elevated stands in the treetops. If we are bowhunters we may need to lower the draw weight of our bows; maybe shorten our effective shot distances because of our inability to practice because of pain or whatever; maybe even limit our hunts closer to home. But we're still out there hunting, absorbing nature and participating. We need to come to the realization we will likely not be able to hunt mountain sheep when we're eighty. And accept the fact we can no longer hike deep into the Rocky Mountains with a 70 lb. pack on our backs, BUT we can maybe hire a guide/outfitter, or beg a younger friend or relative to help us some. We can also adapt a little and hunt elk on less vertical terrain. We could also sit a tree stand over a waterhole and still hear the scream of the herd bull at pink light. Yes, we must adapt, but we're still in the game. That's why golf has a senior circuit.

Additionally, I look at hunting as an individual endeavor versus a team sport. In recent years I've seen hunters referred to as athletes. I don't know, maybe as an individual, but not as a team. I've never thought of hunting as a team sport really. Because we normally all go our separate ways in the morning, your hunting camp partners really aren't your teammates. Just because you drive a Chevy doesn't mean you're the Heartbeat of America, nor does driving a Dodge mean you're Ram Tough either.

There's a big difference between being on a team and going alone. I want to make it clear there's nothing wrong with team sports. Watching a group of individuals work together as a finely tuned unit is impressive, but I don't think they face the same pressures of individual athletes. Maybe I'm wrong. My niece's father-in-law won a Gold Medal at the Tokyo Olympics back in the '60s. He was part of the four-man relay team that brought home the Gold for America that year. I teased him saying, "well YOU actually didn't win the gold, your team did. I mean, if you won the 100-meter sprint yourself or something, I'd be impressed but..." He still likes me (I think) because he knows I was joking/ teasing him.

Hunting is mostly an individual sport. When I was younger, I used to make hunting videos. You can get the best footage by having a cameraman film you. The normal set-up includes a cameraman filming/taping over your shoulder. Twice the scent, twice the bulk to hide; twice the noise; twice the movement; twice the work is involved. But the cameraman can pan and follow the deer as it moves; zoom in and out with telephoto and wide-angle; center the picture, making sure everything is in focus, change the lighting, etc... Filming yourself is really tough. We've always said, either you're a cameraman or a hunter. Trying to be both is really difficult and it shows. Occasionally, filming yourself will work out but not very often. There's a huge difference in capturing lesser quality footage just to show your friends and family, versus trying to capture professional quality production footage. That was the main reason I stopped making production videos for years. I'd plan the entire scenario, set up realizing you're dealing with wild animals here and you'll likely only get one opportunity. Here he comes... finally! Two more steps and he'll be broadside at fifteen yards. And all of a sudden, the cameraman sneezes. I can handle it if I mess up. I know this is likely shrink material here, but I can't handle it when someone else messes me up. You get my drift. Therefore, in more recent years, IF I decide to film, I'll film myself. If I get the scene... great. If I don't... so be it. I'm a hunter first and a cameraman second. Not to mention should I happen to miss on film/tape, when alone I can erase it and no one knows the difference. Coincidentally, I haven't missed it since I dropped people filming me.

Hunting has the unique attribute of being both an individual and a team sport. Frankly, I prefer to hunt alone. If I want to sit all day I can. If I want to go home and take a nap, I can. If I should screw up no one know about it. That happened once to me in 1978 but I don't want to talk about it.

But frankly, hunting with a partner is more fun. Not only will you be an inspiration for each other, i.e., "Hey... I think we need to sit longer this morning" but two heads are better than one. When we talk over a situation it's mentally gratifying to hear someone else's opinion either for another option or to justify your own thinking. Consider what other people say, even if just an inexperienced kid.

Not to mention the safety factor involved. Accidents do happen. When dealing with the elements of nature you always have to consider hypothermia. It's way more deadly than most people give it credit for. Almost everyone I know has fallen regardless of their experience. I've personally had to crawl out of the woods twice myself and both times I was hunting alone. Hunting with a friend or two won't guarantee your safety but it will guarantee someone knows exactly where you are.

Anymore, if I should happen to be hunting alone, I ALWAYS leave a note on the table at home saying the time/date and which stand or area I'm hunting. I also make designated plans to call someone, be it my wife, relative or neighbor, at a specific time after dark so they know I got out of the woods okay. If I fail to call, someone knows where to start looking. Laying out in the elements while hurting all night in freezing temperatures is deadly. We owe it to our families to be responsible.

Often when I hunt, I start as a "team" (one or maybe two other guys) then split up when we leave the vehicle, each going our own ways. So, it's a combination of teamwork and individualism. Half the fun is sharing the adventures with others. Not only do you get to hear their stories firsthand but you also get to share your tales right away. How many times I can remember thinking, "I can't WAIT" to tell someone about what just happened or what I saw. In the last few years though I've noticed when my hunting partner picks me up after dark I now tend to say, "You first... I'm out of breath."

CHAPTER XV
BENIGN

Occasionally a circumstance occurs in life that appears to be little more than a great memory, until you look back on it later. Only then do you realize it was a significant part of the end result. So, it was with this buck.

I passed him up in early November 2012 on film at twelve yards because he had a giant tumor on his chest. The tumor was about the size of an elongated watermelon. It was tough to let him walk but I figured he'd taste terrible. He was a beauty in his prime. I had his left shed from 2011. His G2 measured 13 5/8". I figured they'd probably go 14 inches in 2012. I'm not sure if he had a bad year or due to the tumor/health issues or what, but they were "only" 13 inches in 2012. Brother Gene's trail camera pictures showed he made it through the gun seasons and a long winter.

By fall the watermelon sized tumor had shrunk up to about the size of a small grapefruit or a softball. Obviously, the tumor was not malignant, so I nick-named him "Benign" ... even though he be eight. (Get it?)

On November 8, 2013, I had a perfect wind for the same stand I passed him up from the previous year. I know a lot of people would be shocked if they saw the stand set-up. It's a double tree where the one half apparently got struck by lightning as it snapped off and hanging down at a mere eight feet up. I purposely kept the ladder low in order to blend in with the mass of the doubled trunk. Otherwise, if I was any higher, I'd risk being sky lined. I bet my feet aren't 10 feet off the ground. Even so, I can't ever remember getting busted, so it apparently works fine. The name of the sand is "Buckshot", and it has given me many great memories in past years.

Right at first light I had a single, mature doe go by; then ten minutes later a doe and a yearling; then ten minutes later a 100-inch 4x4 from another direction just out cruising. This was more like it because frankly the season had been slow so far. A short while later I looked to the east and saw him coming. I put the binoculars on him to verify it was him. He was not on the main trail like he was "supposed" to be (imagine that!) but was slightly back in the brush about 20 yards where he had a little more security cover.

At one point he started to angle away from me. If he continued in that direction, I wouldn't get the shot. I thought about wheezing but I really don't like to wheeze when they're that close. If he got out there about fifty yards or so I could wheeze him back in. So, as I often do, more so than a lot of hunters, I let the situation play out rather than have him come looking for me. The Good Lord was on my side... prayers answered! All of a sudden, he turned and walks right to me.

There's a single cedar tree that's about as big around as your thigh about twenty yards south of my stand. I had a steady 5 MPH wind from the south that was perfect. He walked up to the cedar and started to rub it. Now, bear in mind I'm videotaping all this. I slowly swung the camera arm to center him. It was set on wide angle. Just as I started to zoom in, he looked my direction. It was just too big of a gamble. All he had to do was take a couple steps forward and he'd be right in my shooting lane. I'm right-handed. In order to zoom in, I'd have to switch my bow from my left hand to my right hand (the camera was screwed to the tree on my left side that morning), zoom it in, then switch it back to my left shooting hand again. We have to remember what the camera/lens sees is not necessarily the same angle I am seeing, even though I'm only a couple feet away. Every time I'd consider zooming in, he'd coincidentally look my direction. I'm confident, through his body language, he never actually saw me but was only glancing my direction.

Then, I also had to consider if I zoomed in, I'd also have to zoom back out to capture the shot. Sorry but I didn't like the odds and just left it on wide-angle. He rubbed that single tree for seven straight minutes as I filmed. This was not an educated guess on the time as the camera timer recorded it all digitally. Seven minutes is a very long time for a buck to work over a single rub. It's also a very long time for anyone to stand there on red alert knowing what was about to happen at any second. Don't misunderstand me, I'm not complaining as these are memories we will recall the rest of our lives and one of the primary reasons we do this.

Finally, he took one step backwards, pawed the ground a few swipes with each front hoof, brought his tarsals together, peed over his hocks, then slowly started to walk from my left to right. As soon as he entered my shooting lane, I plugged him. The shot was nineteen yards as a "slow walker." My arrow hit a couple inches to the right of where I wanted but it was apparent I instantly broke his beefy right shoulder.

For those of you who are interested in these things, I was shooting my 58 inch Tall Tines takedown recurve that pulls 61 pounds at 28". I was shooting a total arrow weight of 630 grains, a skinny carbon shaft with a 125-grain steel insert and a

One of Benign's massive rubs

125 grain Wensel Woodsman, 3-blade broadhead. The arrow blasted right through his right shoulder and stopped on the far shoulder blade. He peeled out but I instantly knew he was a goner. As he ran off, at about fifty yards I saw him break off the back of the arrow. I'll tell you right now it was pretty intense standing there on red alert for over ten minutes trying to be

patient.

After a few minutes, I gathered my stuff, quietly climbed down and walked over to take some footage of his giant rub. It's pretty impressive. It's one of those giant rubs you'd go out of your way to look at. Just before I shot the 2011 big buck I nicknamed Hurley, he rubbed a big cedar as well. I ended up getting Hurley mounted as a pedestal mount and used his last rub as the upright of the pedestal. Benign's rub is much more impressive. It's one of those rubs if you happened upon, you'd say to yourself, "I'd like to see the buck who made that one."

My plan was to quietly wander over and check the broken arrow/blood and proceed from there, dependent on my findings. When I found the rear 1/3 of the arrow there was plenty of blood. The fact that it'd been twenty minutes and I could see where he was falling in the leaves, I proceeded on. I broke out the camcorder again and taped myself following his blood trail. Maybe a hundred yards later, there was his white belly where he lay. Thank you God!

He died right in the bottom of a dry seepage just downhill of the header I was standing guard over. Now, you know how I'm always having weird stuff happen to me? As I walked up to him, two feet in front of his nose was something laying in the leaves. I said outload to the camera, "What do we have here?" Picking it up, it's one of those aluminum foil helium balloons that said, "HAPPY BIRTHDAY" on it.

Hey, I'll tell you right now if it said, "GET WELL SOON" I would have freaked out!

Now, get this, on a sidenote... 24 hours later, my good friend Daryl Kempher, from Michigan happened to fill a doe tag with his bow. She only made it 50 yards. When he walked up to her laying on the ground right next to her was another one of those foil helium balloons but it was a big Smiley Face! Additionally, on November 30th another good friend, Mike Mitten killed a great 5x4 buck in Illinois. When he walked up to it, there laying on the ground was yet another foil helium party balloon! So that's Iowa, Michigan and Illinois. Think of the chances of that happening. I'll tell you something, I'm seriously thinking of releasing a bunch more of those foil balloons around my hunting areas. I'm looking for investors.

Anyway, he's a beautiful buck and I'm proud of him. As I checked him over, all of a sudden, I realized he broke his left brow tine off. Give me a break (no pun intended)! I don't really care, but I still looked around on his death run and at the bottom of his rub tree and found nothing. He might have broken it off the day before since it was a fresh break.

For those who care, as is (with the broken tine) he measures 157 5/8". If I match the broken tine with the opposing brow tine, (7 2/8") he'd measure 163 2/8" as a 4x4. Almost 26" main beams, 13" G2; 9 3/8" G3s, etc. That's a great 4x4 anywhere.

Now, the rest of the story. He was going to be really tough to get out. I really didn't want to cut him in half, so I called my brother, Gene, who was a hundred miles away in another tree. I told him I'd get it done alone but I wanted someone to know where my body would be lying if I had the big one. Ten minutes later he called back saying he was on his way. Ha... it worked!

Benign on the ground, with a missing brow tine

We literally had to cut our way down the mountain to get the four-wheeler close enough to him. It was embarrassing how many times (six) it took two old guys to just lift him up onto the rack of the four-wheeler (212 lbs. dressed.) I miss my youth. I

Happy and exhausted

ended up taking him into the meat processor for their professional opinion on the tumors.

As mentioned earlier the tumor had deflated substantially since the year prior. It was now about the size of a grapefruit rather than a watermelon. But just to the rear of the tumor there's a prominent scab that is maybe 4 inches long by 2 inches

Benign

Get well soon?

wide with no obvious infection. I'm of the opinion that the big tumor got punctured and drained. I wouldn't be at all surprised he lanced the giant growth while jumping a barbed wire fence and it drained.

The butcher guys said if there was any question on the meat

A look at the lanced tumor

they would discard it. They also mentioned they saw similar tumors on a lot more critters than people know about. Either way, I ate him and here it is years later and I'm still kicking, although my neck seems to swell in November.

My apology on the included photos I know I'm not smiling but I was already whipped. Let me put it this way, I shot the buck at 7:56 AM and we finally got him out at 5PM. I'm smiling on the inside!

CHAPTER XVI

PICKING RIPE FRUIT

It seems half the fun of hunting is sharing with those who understand, especially when the adventure ends in success. It's like we're all a bunch of dudes with the same disease or psychological disorder and can relate to each other.

I have to admit 2010 was an outstanding season for me. It seemed no matter what I did or where I hunted, I bumped into nice bucks. Most of you know I am very picky when it comes to whitetails. My goals may seem ridiculous to some but it's just personal and that's what I prefer. As a resident of Iowa, we are allowed one buck in the general bow season. We cannot shoot a second buck until after the general gun season when we are then allowed to hunt with our bows during the late muzzleloader season. I prefer to bow hunt. I don't even own a muzzleloader, or a shotgun for that matter. That means if I should shoot a buck in early October, I cannot bowhunt for a second buck until right around Christmas. That means no buck hunting in October, November and most of December. Frankly, I'm getting too old to sit out most of the fall without a valid buck tag in my pocket. And with a limited income and our economy I can't afford out-of-state trips, gas/fuel, motels and costly non-resident deer licenses.

My brother and I have limited ourselves to about the same goals annually. I want a fully mature buck of at least 5.5 years old, approximately 160 inches of antler and under the 20-yard line. I know this might sound ridiculous and make some people

Meltdown on the hoof

jealous but I've tried to pattern my whole life to be able to do what I do. And yes, it's taken a lot of sacrifice in more ways than one.

On October 28, 2009, I missed the buck I nicknamed Hurley. I got multiple trail camera photos of him in the early fall of 2010 so he was my main objective. There were probably even higher measured bucks around, but I wanted Hurley for personal reasons and because I had history with him.

I had several stands set up especially for Hurley but I tried to intelligently hunt him only with perfect winds and sparingly so as not to pressure him out of his area.

In October of 2010 I passed up four bucks I thought would measure around 150 inches waiting for Hurley. One was named "Holyfield" because he had a big chunk out of his left ear. He was a standing 7x6. Another we nicknamed "Meltdown" because his one main beam drooped down on the end like a melted candle. He was a standing 6x5, but both my brother and I agreed they were each only 4.5 yrs. old and if given one more year would likely both become B&C class bucks when they were finally fully mature.

In mid-October I had Holyfield walk by me at 5:15 PM with the sun shining on him in all his glory. I filmed him making four scrapes, doing the overhead branch routine, rubbing, peeing on his hocks, etc. at eighteen yards. In the days to follow I also passed him up at 15 yds. and 12 yards.

The morning after my first close confrontation with Holyfield I sat in the stand I missed Hurley from in 2009. At 8 AM Meltdown followed a doe with a pretty face and hung around at sixteen yards for a solid ten minutes. I got great video footage. The future for these two great bucks was looking bright.

On Saturday morning, October 30th things were really heating up. I saw eight bucks and twelve does by noon. I filmed a nice 5x5 that followed a doe right under me at four yards. Life was great!

That afternoon the winds were out of the southwest but were predicted to switch out of the northwest later that afternoon. I wanted to keep out of Hurley's core area for a couple days because I felt I may be pushing him a little too much. I chose shifting to a stand we called "The Tennessee Bottoms" on a different farm about five miles away. It's a great stand for both southwest or northwest winds. It's located about halfway into the stand I killed a nice 6x5 from the previous year. As soon as I crossed the fence into the bottoms, I knew my timing was right. The entire area was absolutely torn up with big, fresh rubs and scrapes. It looked like a bomb had gone off.

And I hadn't hunted it yet that year so everything was smokin' fresh.

About 5 PM it was like someone opened the gate. Between 5PM and 6PM I'd already seen four bucks and NO does. A spikehorn, two 4x4s and a medium 5x5. At about 6:10 a very nice, mature 5x5 came in from over my left shoulder from the south. He walked right past me at 12 yards. I didn't dare turn the camera on for fear of spooking him and blowing the entire area up. I now feel this was a major decision on my part. After he got out there a way, I took some safe footage and watched him walk away, then hung the camera back up. I kept looking behind him in case something was following. A couple minutes later movement caught my eye through the foliage. There was a great one! "My man" was up on his hind legs working the overhead branch of a scrape I had seen earlier.

I grabbed for the camcorder, but just as I was turning it on, he dropped down, freshened the scrape and here he comes right to me. Being only fifty yards and advancing on me I had no time to film... sorry folks.

As his head went behind a tree I stood up, when his head went behind another tree I took the bow from the bow-hook. You know how when you're in a stand you choose your "sweet spot"? That's where, if you had your choice, you'd most like your buck to be standing. Well, he walked right into my sweet spot, broadside at 13 yards, stopped and turned his head directly away from me. It was like it was meant to be.

In all honesty, I hesitated a little because I had my heart set on Hurley. But this was just too good of a 4x4 to let him walk, and too perfect of a shot. I lost self-control.

I was shooting a brand-new, custom Tall Tines takedown recurve from my good friend Brian Wessel (not Wensel), of Keokuk, Iowa. The bow was a virgin that season. For those interested, it was a 58-inch length, 61 lbs. at 28" beauty with a riser of Bolivian Rosewood and limbs of Black Limba. The bow just "fits", feels right to me and shoots great.

I know this is hard to believe, but of the hundreds of big game animals I've bow-killed over the years I never have spine-shot a single animal. When I shot, in my mind's eye, the arrow placement looked a little high but not much. I was absolutely shocked and unprepared when he dropped right in his tracks!

Not to elaborate on a place a lot of us have been, I finished him off as soon as I could. Climbing down from my perch and standing next to him was a feeling I'll remember for the rest of my life. Sometimes, we have "ground shrinkage" when first approaching a big critter. But this was the exact opposite. The closer I got the bigger he looked. Thank you Lord!

Maybe it was God's way of not letting me get too sure of myself because I hadn't even touched him yet when panic set in. What sounded like less than 100 yards from me, three coyotes blasted off yipping and howling. I never saw them but I mean they were right there downwind of me. I'm not sure if they smelled blood and were trying to spook me off, or if it was just coincidental. But reality struck, I was alone with no side-arm, three broadheads and a blunt left. I did not want to leave my giant buck for a second.

The creek bottom I needed to cross in order to get him out was washed out deep from many decades of rains and flooding. The shear walls from the top to the bottom were thirty feet straight down, a twenty-foot span of gravel bottom and another thirty feet straight back up the other side. Absolutely no way! In fact, my brother and I have a rope tied to a tree at the easiest place to cross so we could lower ourselves down and pull ourselves back up the other side if needed. But that would be if I was alone, not dragging a 230 lb. plus buck out.

The creek itself basically runs East/west. I knew the banks were even steeper to the west so after field-dressing him I tried dragging my buck on the north shelf to the east towards a spot I thought I might be able to get him across. I only made it about 75 yards and I was physically out of gas. Either I'm getting too old for this stuff or this buck was bigger than I thought... or both.

I'm a little embarrassed about what I ended up doing in my panicked mode. My brother was over a hundred miles away and hunting by himself. I couldn't physically get the buck out myself but I also didn't want to leave him for the coyotes. So, I ended up stripping myself of clothing. I draped every piece of clothing I had over the carcass. Shirts, jackets, sweatshirts, tee-shirts, hats, vests, handkerchiefs, gloves, socks, etc. Because I was sweating like a pig, I wiped myself off with each article of clothing before I draped them over the carcass like a big ol' grizz after a fresh kill. Then, I reluctantly walked out almost naked. No... I kept my dirty undies on. But I was sure glad I didn't bump into another bowhunter while walking out or on the road.

I didn't sleep too well that night. After a few telephone calls I found out a good friend, Daryl Kempher from Michigan, was on his way to hunt a farm in Iowa about fifty miles away. He offered to help me drag him out so I took him up on it. Ironically, the exact same scenario happened two years prior when Daryl was on his way to a hunt in Kansas and he helped me drag out another 160 incher.

Gene couldn't get there till that afternoon, so Daryl and I pulled him out. In that circus Daryl fell down the side of the steep cliff/embankment while we were crossing. He landed hard and was rolling around on the ground in severe pain. I thought for sure he'd broken his shoulder. So, here's a guy who finally drew an Iowa non-resident tag after anxiously waiting three years and he then injures himself the day before his hunt was to start. We didn't know if he could even draw his bow. Then he said, "don't worry about it… I'll draw that bow if I have to draw it with my teeth." My kind of guy!

After a hot shower, a few healthy over-doses of Ibuprofen and a good night's sleep, I was pleased to hear he was much better.

We finally got the buck near the truck when my brother called saying he was on his way. Daryl took off for his hunt and I waited for Gene's arrival. I just sat there staring and thanking the Lord not only for my great buck, but for my great life, my health, my family and friends.

Upon Gene's arrival we took some great walk-up footage to share with family and friends, but then had a really hard time trying to load him into the back of my truck ourselves. I'm telling you, I'm jealous of you young guys anymore… but I'm not complaining.

After I caped the buck I found out he'd recently been in a wicked fight. He had deep puncture wounds all the way from his brisket to his throat. You know how when you peel the cape from the carcass how the tissue is just normally muscle and fascia? Well, this guy was all bloodshot, infected and actually smelled sour.

I had him mounted by my friend and world-class taxidermist Tony Grillo, of Seymour, Indiana. I sent the cape frozen, next-day delivery and the hide still slipped, I'm certain due to the local infection. Brian Wessel to the rescue again. He had an extra cape in his freezer. Great friends are a real blessing.

I'd like to see the buck who put the whooping on mine. For those who are interested in measurements, he taped 173 3/8" gross and netted 169 4/8" as a basic 4x4/ eight point. His G2s were 13 3/8" and 13"; G3s were a foot each and he had an outside spread of 24 inches. A 140" 4x4 is a good one; a 150" 4x4 is a really good one; a 160" 4x4 is outstanding, so it gives one some idea of how really rare a 170-inch class 4x4 really is.

After scrutinizing some old video footage, we realized Gene and I both had passed up my buck in 2007 because he had a broken right brow tine and we guessed he was only 4.5 yrs. old. We didn't see him to our knowledge when he was 5.5 or 6.5 yrs. old so we assumed he was 7.5 yrs. old when I got him

This account wouldn't be complete if I didn't fill in the rest of the story. My Iowa tag was filled on October 30, 2010. Because I didn't have another valid buck tag until late December, I pretty much hunted the remainder of the season with just my video camcorder. The bad news is I developed some serious camera problems when I needed it the most. The last time this happened I had to send it away for repair to the tune of $845. And I didn't receive it back for a month, so I tried to adapt.

On November 5th I had an absolutely great day. I sat a stand we named "Ringer" from light until dark and recorded a total of

Nearly a 170" basic 8-point

seven different bucks in the morning and three more in the afternoon. At about 4:15 PM up walked an absolutely beautiful 5x5, that we'd previously nick-named "Split Ear", that would measure around 170 inches. If I had a valid tag, I would have absolutely taken him in a heartbeat and added another potential Booner to my wall.

He walked up to the scrape I was standing guard over and did the whole rutting ritual at 18 yards. Just as I tried to film him all of a sudden, the view finder started to flash, "EJECT CASSETTE!" I got the tape out and put it back in. I was amazed I got away with all the clicking, buzzing and whirring. But alas, when I tried to tape him again, I got the same warning indicating dirty heads in the camera. Old Split Ear walked away totally unaware this was his lucky day. A Booner, totally oblivious at 18 yards in good light. And I didn't have a valid buck tag, nor a camera that would

Trail camera photo of Picket

give me a lick of footage.

Later that night I blew the camera out with a can of compressed air and ran through two different sets of head cleaners to hopefully help me temporarily correct the problem. It "seemed" to fix it.

The next afternoon I chose a stand we call "Old Yeller". About 3:30, with the sun shining, a string of five does came right to me, followed by the man himself... Hurley. The girls got right in front of me and locked up. Although I had a perfect wind, they knew something wasn't right. They were 25 yds. from me. There was Hurley standing broadside right in the open at 40 yds. in all His glory with the sun shining on him and I couldn't make a move to turn the camera on without the whole scene blowing up. But I had to try... it was too beautiful.

I slowly raised the camera up and hit the record button only to see, "EJECT CASSETTE". You gotta be kidding me! I tried to do it as quietly as possible but the entire group was spooked. In the turmoil I ejected the tape and replaced it in time to get a good solid two seconds of footage as he crested the horizon. What a disappointment. Stay tuned, it gets better.

Fifteen minutes later, four does and a spikehorn headed right for me, followed by one we nicknamed "Picket". What a gorgeous buck he was! He was a wide, symmetrical, standing 6x6 typical that would have measured in the 180s. An absolute, no questions asked, Boone and Crockett typical buck in his prime.

The four does and the spike he was following crossed the old fence and walked right under me, three on my right and two on my left at five yards. The camera was temporarily working and I got some poor footage of Picket working a scrape at about fifty yards. Then he turned and walked towards me. He was behind the leaves of an overhanging limb but I could see him doing his thing to another scrape I wasn't even aware was there, at maybe 20 yds. He needed to take about two more steps and I would be getting world-class footage of a B&C buck at under 20 yards. I was ready.

I know people aren't going to believe this but, as I've said dozens of times before, weird stuff just seems to happen to me. My cell phone in my chest pocket went off! Yes, it was on vibrate… but he still heard it. He just stood there looking around. The phone stopped buzzing. Maybe I was going to get away with this. The thought just crossed my mind when that little ringy, dingy, chime thingy tune/ jingle went off that tells me someone just left me a message. He EXPLODED out of there obviously not liking the jingle.

By the way, it was my beautiful daughter from Montana calling to tell me she missed me and loved me. What can I say? I later returned her call and told her I missed and loved her as well, but please try not to love me so much in November.

Two days later after more camera first aid, I sat a stand we named "Triple By-Pass" with the camcorder. Sitting in the ladder with the camera in my lap, I looked up to see a beautiful bobcat walking right to me through the hardwoods. When he got right below me, he suddenly sat down and scratched behind his ear with his hind leg. Super footage but the camera AGAIN starts flashing "EJECT CASSETTE". I was going through the all too familiar ritual when additional movement caught my eye. It was Hurley. He glanced over at the bobcat as he walked by at 25 yds. Again, not a lick of footage! You gotta be kidding me!

The year ended with me seeing Hurley a total of six times. I "passed up" Holyfield four times; Meltdown twice; as well as Split-Ear and Picket. What more could a guy ask for? I'm very blessed.

I've always tried to preach, when relating to whitetail bucks, not to pick the fruit until it's ripe. Now I need to consider when it gets over-ripe, falls from the tree and rots. But... it was a great game and we all win some and lose some.

"A deer lives and dies based on messages received from its nose"

CHAPTER XVII
CLOSING THE DEAL

After missing the buck I called Hurley in 2009 I continued my pursuit onward. At the end of the 2010 season, I had seen Hurley in the timber a total of six times. And, I had gotten multiple trail camera pictures to whet my appetite, many even in broad daylight. I don't use trail camera pictures to "pattern" a deer but I do use them for entertainment purposes and to add fuel to the burning fire.

I'm not sure of the reasoning, but Hurley appeared to have dropped a good 25 pounds in body weight in 2010 when he should have been 8.5 years old. He was still running the ridges but he was getting old. With the weight loss I feared he wouldn't make the upcoming winter. But he was a survivor.

It appeared my quest would continue but not without concerns. I found trespassing human boot prints right in the middle of Hurley's core area. I heard rumors of local folks seeing him from the road. I often heard gunfire from the fringes of his home turf. I got nervous when watching slow driving vehicles and road hunters at dawn or dusk, wondering if their intentions were honorable.

Our trail cameras revealed Hurley would be around for the 2011 season. He was looking even older, entering that fall at 9.5 years.

On October 22, 2011, I was walking out after dark on a little skid road where I'd seen Hurley several times before. The leaves

Hurley

were damp as I quietly proceeded back to my truck with flashlight in hand. As I rounded a slight bend something caught my eye ahead. It was in the exact same spot I had seen Hurley cross once the year before, and where previous close examination revealed a minor trail. I could see two widely spaced, slightly reflective eyes watching me. Bringing my binoculars up I could just barely see antlers in the low light... big antlers! I just knew it was him. Immediately turning the light out, I just stood there in silence since I had a favorable wind. I gave him plenty of time. I wanted him to move on hopefully

A younger Hurley

without disturbance. I'm of the opinion that when its dark outside, deer think they're invisible. You can get away with a lot more under the cover of darkness.

A couple mornings later on my way into a stand in the dark, I found a fresh scrape right where his minor trail crossed the skid road. Hurley made very aggressive, concave scrapes pawed deeply into the ground. I was almost certain it was his scrape. I had yet another clue to dwell on.

The very next morning, October 29th, as Gene and I walked the skid road before light, I pointed out the fresh scrape to my brother. Gene mentioned he had a trail camera in his backpack but because we were running a little late, he just laid it on the ground pointing towards the overhead branch of the scrape, turned it on and we walked away.

This is interesting stuff that all adds to the story. That morning I never saw a deer... zero. Gene saw two does from his stand. On the way out for lunch he pulled the SD card from the camera we'd placed going in that morning. An hour later it revealed a giant bodied buck standing in the scrape. You couldn't see the head in the frame but I thought I recognized that body. Another piece of the puzzle slid into place. That made three times I thought he'd crossed there. I needed to get a stand up!

Mid-morning of October 30th, I scrutinized the area. This particular habitat is made up of mature hardwood timber with minimal understory, making it visually scenic yet hard to read. I could see the ground well, but I had to rely on terrain features more than sign. It all made sense. The skid road runs basically east/west. To the north is a little flat covered with tight whips/saplings and slash, then a bowl dropping down into a creek bottom far below. Sign indicated Hurley was habitually coming around the bowl from the north in the morning, crossing the skid road to follow the little finger ridge south, down into the bottom, crossing that creek bed in order to bed on the north facing slope with predominant south winds covering his back. This way, he entered his bedding area with a headwind, positioning himself to watch his back-trail in the open hardwoods as the southerly wind covered his rear and warming daytime thermals drifted up to him from north to south. This was absolutely textbook, common sense on his part but details we as humans often overlook.

The fact it was clean, "pretty woods" became a problem. I didn't want to get too far south near his primary bedding area because his exact travel pattern varied. I needed to concentrate where I knew he was coming through. I found a decent tree in a good location but it really wasn't what I wanted. But, as I've preached dozens of times, I much prefer a mediocre tree in a great location over a great tree in a mediocre spot. The tree was only maybe fourteen inches in diameter, not the best size to hide a big guy. But there was a slightly smaller tree just off my left shoulder and another decent size tree a few feet behind that would help break up my outline. Then, I also wired a few more extra leafy branches to give me even more cover at critical angles. It would work.

I then got sneaky. The minor trail he was using passed at about twenty yards. Shooting a recurve bow instinctively, I'm a fifteen-yard guy. So, with the inverted blade of my pole-pruner and my trusty hoe, I whisked a new, more visible trail in the dry leaves that angled just slightly closer to my stand creating more of a visual to catch his eye. Then I laid a five-inch diameter deadfall branch just west of his north/south trail, angling it just enough to hopefully nudge his travel routine to fifteen yards rather than twenty.

I also added a mock scrape on my new trail and sweetened it with Smokey's excellent doe-in-heat and pre-orbital scents. I named the stand "Goner" because of his passing by the morning of October 29th while we were gone. The trap was set.

I needed a southwest wind to hunt the stand best. Please bear with me on these details as they all add up and are vitally important on why it ultimately worked out. The morning of October 31st I got a southwest wind at 8 MPH. As if it was meant to be, we also got the first hard frost of the year that I always talk about. It consistently always is one of the best hunting days of the season... bar none. Remember that! The cold snap that night dropped the temperature to a frosty 24 degrees. Perfect... absolutely perfect.

Remembering the day before I never saw a single deer, it was like someone flipped the switch. I'm telling you, that first hard frost of the season can be a real game changer! That day I saw a total of 39 deer, including seven racked bucks. Deer were running and chasing all around me. I passed up one buck pushing 150 inches as he chop-stepped a hot doe twelve yards in front of me. But not Hurley, not even a glimpse.

The morning of November 1, 2011, dawned clear but the temps warmed up to the mid-40s during the night with predictions of higher temps later in the day. Once again, I had my preferred southwest winds at maybe 8MPH. I seldom sit a stand two days in a row, but because of perfect stand placement and wind/deer angles, I felt I really didn't taint the area much on the previous all-day hunt. Things were just too perfect... like it was meant to be.

Again, I've always liked a wind that was "almost wrong" as long as it was directionally consistent. Sign indicated Hurley had been angling in from the NNW across the skid road, then heading due south to his bedding area. The SSW wind would give him the false sense of security of a nose wind. Again, the stage was set. It just felt right. I've always learned to trust and go by your gut feelings.

At 8:38 AM I hadn't seen a single deer yet. It just goes to show you how the temperature change can affect movement and hamper the chasing. By 8:38 the previous morning I'd probably already seen 15 or 18 deer. But have faith, stay tuned.

Movement suddenly caught my eye across the skid road to the northwest. I could just barely see him taking his last strokes on a 6" diameter cedar. Then, here he comes, all alone, walking right to me and headed to his bedroom. My heart seemed to be beating faster and louder. I reminded myself to take long, deep breaths. It was gonna happen.

He stopped at his scrape just off the road, sniffed without pawing and walked in on the new trail I'd created myself. Another "thank you Lord" and another quick prayer. I immediately turned the camcorder on, pointing it where I knew the shot was going to be. Hitting the record button, I watched the little red light go on, indicating it was recording. Now, the bad news; I saw the red light go on but whether it didn't catch or whether I double clicked it in the excitement when taking my finger off the trigger doesn't really matter. The fact remains, my camera shut down without me knowing it. As I've said before, either you're a hunter or a videographer but being both is really tough.

Hurley walked in on my new trail perfectly until he got to the downed branch I'd positioned to shift him a little closer to me. When he got to the limb, rather than coming closer, he stepped

The treestand, with appropriate back cover, from where Hurley was standing

to his right, going around the far side of the barrier. That was my bad, in that if I laid it two feet farther west it would have made all the difference in the world to his direction of travel. He angled slightly quartering away for a few steps, heading into the southwest wind, then turned broadside walking slowly right to

Hurley on the ground

left at about 20 yards. I didn't dare try to stop him. I thought if I did, he'd be looking and might bust me in the smallish tree I was in. As I've done for years, I timed my shot while he slowly walked. He never knew what hit him.

The arrow blew right through his giant body and disappeared. In my mind's eye, I saw a good hit, but shortly thereafter I started second guessing myself. Maybe it was just slightly back. What if it was lower than I thought and I only paunched him? Because of the heavy foliage I lost sight of him in just ten yards or so. Because my mind was playing tricks on me, I wasn't absolutely positive of the hit and surely didn't want to jump him if he was nearby. I decided to play it safe and stay on stand until noon.

Finally, I got down and quietly walked over expecting to find my arrow... but there was nothing. No arrow, no hair, no blood, no evidence whatsoever. I quietly backed out with the intention of going home, reviewing the footage and assessing the hit.

Admiring Hurley up close

When I discovered no footage, I decided to again play it safe by postponing the search until 3PM. Even though it got up to 81 degrees that afternoon. With no blood or spent arrow, I figured maybe the feathers hung up on the exit plugging the hole.

At 3PM we weren't on the trail for two minutes when I

looked up to see Hurley's white belly lying dead about 75 yards from where I shot. Thank you again, Lord! I instantly had very mixed feelings. I had attained my goal, my dream, yet it suddenly seemed too final. I kept thinking I was going to suddenly wake up to find it was all just a dream. I was honestly all choked up. But I then started smiling to myself knowing this would always go down as one of the highest points of my long hunting life.

For those interested in statistics, Hurley field-dressed 248 pounds at the meat locker and measured 190 1/8 inches as a 7x7. He was well past his prime. As I previously stated, last year I noticed he dropped maybe 25 pounds in body weight and his rack went downhill with age. This year he actually grew a basic 5x5 frame, whereas in previous seasons he had a 5x4 frame but with more and longer non-typical points. I suspect he was 9.5 years old because of previous sightings and all the history I had with him all the way back to 2006.

Just prior to crossing the skid road where I killed him, Hurley hit what I call his "last rub". It's a six-inch diameter cedar that he'd obviously worked over many times before. Something suddenly clicked in my head and I got a brainstorm. I cut down Hurley's last rub out of respect and decided to use it as the upright for his pedestal mount. I thought it would be fitting. Friend and world-class taxidermist Dennis Behn is a head sculptor for McKenzie taxidermy forms. He mounted Hurley on a beautiful new line of whitetail mannequins for me. He even became a "model" in McKenzie's taxidermy-form catalog. The ability to sit back and look at a beautiful creation of such a magnificent animal shows honor and respect forever.

I thank God for making this come together so perfectly.

When a person locates and hunts a specific animal for multiple years, a personal relationship develops whether intended or not. By handicapping myself with a range limited weapon such as a traditional bow, one can't help but feel a special bond during the pursuit. This personal closeness is something I feel a lot of hunters cheat themselves out of in modern times. Because of the intimate relationship that is developed, one senses a loss very similar to the death of a loved one. We must accept these emotions just like we do with other personal losses. Time heals.

Hurley's descendants are out there. Someday, hopefully both you and I will develop a personal relationship with yet another very special whitetail and more dreams will eventually become reality.

"Knowledge is 10%, whereas application of knowledge is 90%"

CHAPTER XVIII
DEAD END

My brother, Gene, used to say, "When on stand when I was younger, I used to stand up until my feet got sore, then I'd sit down. Now that I'm older, I sit until my butt gets sore, then I stand up." I can definitely relate to that.

The name of this particular tree stand is "Dead End." It sits atop a hardwood ridge that basically runs east/west. To the north is a pretty significant bluff that overlooks the lower creek bottom and cultivated crop fields way below. There's an old skid road that runs along the top, the remnants from when the ridge was logged maybe seventy-five years ago. About where the logging road hits the bluff it kind of dead ends. Actually, you can see where the old road used to continue on down over the ridge at a sharp angle but you can barely walk/climb it anymore. You can drive in a four-wheeler from the east but where the old road hits the bluff is about as far as you can go, thus, the "dead end."

Deer can easily walk the edge of the bluff on a predominant south/southwest wind to scent check any activities to the south. If you could see the angles the old logging road makes as it worms its way through the shelves and fingers you would understand the exact stand placement. It's very good when bucks are cruising for does, as well as both morning and evening bedding/feeding natural movements.

It was a midday sit during the last few days of October 2019. Because I only have one buck tag for the general bow season, I'm very picky. But the last few days of October have always been very good to me. I've killed two B&C class bucks just before Halloween in previous years.

A couple hours into the sit, off to my right, here comes a beautiful, fully mature typical 5x5 stud walking right down the logging road. He was all alone on a slight northwest breeze looking for company.

He was clean, wide and handsome. I figured he would measure in the 160s. Certainly a great buck in his prime but I questioned whether I wanted to tag out again in October and miss the main rut. I had my camcorder mounted just to my right. I decided if I could get the kill on tape I'd take him. If not, I'd pass. As he advanced on me with his steady gate, I was having problems with my camcorder. I wanted the angle wide enough to see the shot transpire but zoomed in enough to see the arrow placement. On top of setting that, the auto-focus was going in and out. It's hard to explain because I was relatively calm but I was also in a panic to get the camera properly in my control. No excuses. The shot would be about 20 yards walking right to left. Now, don't forget, I still hadn't decided to shoot him unless I could get him on tape. He was pushing me to rush. The camera was still not right but he was right there standing in front of me begging for it. I suddenly realized he was just too good of a buck to not take... camera or not.

Just then he started walking again, got behind a couple bigger trees and got through my primary shooting lane before I got the camera out of the way. Remember me previously saying you need to either be a videographer or a hunter but being both is really tough? Absolutely no excuses. He made me rush the shot. It was his fault... yeah. I'm going to say he was maybe 22 yards. The shot looked good at first but I watched it drop just

Clean, wide and handsome

under his heart, an absolute clean miss. Not only did I not get the buck but I also didn't get the footage. Yeah... I hadn't missed since 1965... yeah. I remember thinking, "golly gee, gosh darn, son of a gun!" or something like that.

Fast forward until December. Don't hold me to the exact

stats but it was very cold and windy that day. But the wind was consistent, out of the northwest. No problem, I was dressed for it and still had that tag burning a hole in my pocket keeping me warm.

You need to realize the fall foliage had, by now, cleared out most of those last stubborn leaves. Although I was no longer hidden as well, the fifteen-foot ladder was tucked in between two big oaks right beside each other. I felt if I remained sitting, I wouldn't be as likely to move around as much. It's important for me to explain this was a good quality ladder stand with a flip-up metal seat. When you wanted to stand you could get your butt up against the tree for stability. They normally come with a two-inch padded, removeable cushion on the seat. For some reason there wasn't a cushion on this stand. No big deal as I have plenty of "cushioning" on my buttocks.

I entered the stand shortly after noon. As I recall, the temperature was in the upper teens. I hung my recurve on the bow hook and settled in. I never saw a thing all afternoon. Maybe 20 minutes before the end of legal shooting light I heard something coming behind me and to my left. All that time waiting and they caught me off guard. They were under me before I could even lift my bow from the hook. It was a family group of five does and yearlings. They walked by at 12 yards totally unaware. After they cleared, I figured I better stand up so I could be more mobile if a buck was following.

Here comes the hairy part. When I tried to stand up I couldn't. I don't mean I was stiff/ stoved up; I mean I literally COULD NOT stand up. Then I realized I hadn't stood for almost five hours in those cold temperatures. I had not stood up to stretch; didn't stand to pee, etc. The edge of that metal seat had cut into my legs just at the base of my buttocks. Remember the femoral artery folks?

The first thing I did was flex/extend my legs while I remained seated. There wasn't any pain but they felt numb and stiff. I worked them for a long time without standing... maybe five full minutes without even trying to stand up. Finally, I tried to stand but still couldn't make it. I could reach the arm of my bow hook. With the help of my one arm pulling up and the other arm pushing up off the ladder seat, I finally got standing. I then, again, tried flexing/extending my legs, only this time while standing up.

It was hard to explain. I could stand but I couldn't feel my feet at all. The best way to describe it was it felt like I was standing on stilts and couldn't feel the ground. I unsnapped my safety strap and re-snapped it on every rung of the ladder as I carefully, slowly descended. Once on the ground I felt more relieved but things were still not right. I cut a sapling for a walking stick and slowly walked out to my truck. Again, it felt like I was walking on stilts and the walk took me about three times as long as it normally would. Once I got to my truck I even had a hard time climbing in.

The first thing I did when I got home was soak in a bathtub of hot water. I have one of those giant foot massagers that will knock your fillings out even with your shoes on. I also have one of those giant hand-held vibrators that look like a table sander. I bet I vibrated both legs alternately for an hour. I then took a couple aspirins (blood thinners) and went to bed.

The next day I was surprised and concerned I still had a hard time walking. I didn't even hunt. I repeated the massage; hot tub; aspirin routine. I also got on the internet and researched my problem.

This is serious stuff folks. It's a condition known as Deep Vein Thrombosis (DVT). You can actually DIE from it. I somewhat knew about it but it was one of those things you tend to not think about and brush off. It's the reason they suggest people, especially seniors, who are driving/riding long distances to get out of their vehicle every couple hours if only to walk around the car a little.

Another example floored me. As we get older our muscle tone tends to diminish. When we reach our fifties, our gluteal muscles turn to mush. We lose our tonicity. And get this, they said older people who have a habit of sitting on the toilet for long periods reading have been known to develop DVT clots. So... if you happen to be reading this fine book while sitting on the john, head for the recliner instead. You can thank me later!

In my hunting example, without standing up or changing my position sitting in that treestand for five hours straight the edge of the metal seat acted similar to a tourniquet, completely cutting off the circulation to my lower extremities. In essence, the normal blood flow stops and the blood actually starts to clot without "trauma." The clot can create a pulmonary embolism in the pulmonary artery and end up in your lungs. It's very rare at 0.2% but can be fatal. HUH??? Yes, you can have serious potential, life threatening physical problems from just sitting in your treestand. Who woulda thunk? Now aren't you glad you bought this book?

So, be aware. If you intend to sit for long hours in a great tree, make sure to occasionally stand up and stretch. Do a few isometrics when on stand. That too will warm you up a little. Try to keep the blood circulating. That's the whole idea behind this fine book... to give you exciting, close confrontations with giant bucks in order to keep your blood pumping. Try to be like those younger guys my brother speaks of... stand up and only occasionally sit down when your feet get sore. It'll let you live longer.

By the way, I never saw that buck again. Similar to a lot of big bucks, he just disappeared, leaving us with only memories, dreams and knowledge of a few dead ends.

Buck in the fall forest

Same buck, same place, after a snow

CHAPTER XIX
THOUGHTS ON SCRAPES

The study of whitetail deer and their behavior seems to be a puzzle a lot of us fanatics can't seem to understand. What we tend to do is try to understand the social behavior of an animal via our visual encounters of the species and our abilities to reason what we are seeing. We are similar to a bunch of pediatricians trying to diagnose a problem from a screaming baby. It would be so much easier if the baby could tell us where it hurt. In the same respect, think of how much more knowledgeable we would have if we could communicate with each individual animal. Often our theories are a guess at best.

Since I originally penned this piece in 1986, please bear in mind this was "breaking news" back then and this speculation was somewhat ahead of its time. Most of what we read, including this, is personal opinion and supposition. Theories were about the best we could come up with back then. If our theories can be substantiated through consistent success in the hunting field, it gives us a feeling of personal satisfaction in that we just may be correct in our ideas of repetitious positive theories eventually being accepted as fact.

More recently I've been reading a lot of speculation on the function of buck scrapes. In my own opinion most is just a brushing over of the true meaning and function of breeding activities. We hear and read that the function of the scrape is the buck leaving his "calling card" stating he stands ready and able to accomplish the breeding ritual. All well and good, but I personally believe some of our deer biologists that there is a lot more going on than meets the eyes of a casual observer.

The whitetail breeding system differs totally from that of elk for example. Both elk and whitetails are polygynous in that males mate with several females of their species (similar to some guys I know, ha.). But the elk utilize a harem type of system, whereas the whitetail uses a system biologically known as tending bond. With this system the male tends to only one female at a time until she is successfully inseminated.

Because of the one-on-one bonding this is where the true function and necessity of the scrape comes into play. The buck places scrapes throughout his territory where they can best be thought of as an invitation. As we have said in the past, it is the doe that accepts the scrape site near which the future breeding will take place. Knowing a great majority of these factors take place in the dark of night, makes it difficult for us to understand what all is happening.

It's generally debatable if the doe or the buck initially chooses the potential scrape sites in areas they know are frequented by heavier deer activity. Then, I'm of the opinion that the doe picks what is to become the primary breeding scrape for two reasons. First, the location will be strategic in positioning, allowing safe access for both the buck and the doe through thermal evaluation and security. This is why we often find the heaviest rutting sign in some of the thickest covers. You'll often find any excessive rutting sign found in open terrain suggests almost strictly nocturnal use. I've often stated if the scrape hunter is not certain exactly where to set up in the rutting area, he should concentrate his efforts slightly downwind of the most scrapes he can find in the smallest, thickest area. In this way, we know the scrape hunter will at least be within the ballpark and not out in left field... or should I say not "left out in the field?"

Thoughts on Scrapes

Up close on the licking branch

The second and lesser understood reason a doe chooses one scrape over another is her personal evaluation of the sexuality of the individual buck who made/ visited that scrape.

The foundation behind the scrape is strictly scent oriented. Communication between the buck and the doe is strictly through scent until the actual breeding takes place. In more recent years, trail camera and radio telemetry have allowed 24/7 monitoring to answer a lot of previously gray areas for us. Primary scrape odors determine both the personal identification and the physical/ health condition of the two sexes involved strictly through scent.

Let's break down these two functions of the scrape (identification and physical condition of the deer) even more. When the buck urinates over his tarsal glands (the hock glands on the inside of the back legs) urine mixes with glandular buck secretions, runs down the inside of his back leg and is deposited in the scrape itself. The more he rub-urinates the blacker his hock glands will appear. Urine running through the tarsal glands and deposited in the ground/scrape accomplishes two very important things critical to the future of the deer herd. The buck has left his personal identifying odor as well as his physical condition for evaluation by the receptive doe. It's very similar to a male dog making his rounds through the neighborhood peeing, if only a squirt, on every tree and fire hydrant he goes by.

The buck's personal identification has been deposited through the odor of the tarsal gland. It's very important to note this odor is very distinctive from any other buck in the area and denotes the fact he is running this scrape line. Each and every buck within the herd has a different/ distinct odor/aroma. It is similar to how a dairy cow can pick her single calf out of a whole barnyard full of other calves. Each animal has a distinct odor and can identify it amongst the entire herd. After numerous social confrontations within the deer herd, the pecking order,

Thoughts on Scrapes

Making a scrape

etc. throughout the year, the doe knows the distinctly different odor between "Joe the stud" 10-pointer and that ratty little 3-pointer that is constantly bothering her within the herd's social structure.

Obvious confusion on our part comes into play when we

might have upwards of a dozen different bucks hitting a particular breeding scrape. But the confusion is only in our minds... the doe has absolutely no trouble deciphering different individual buck scents deposited in the scrapes. A lot of this is easier to understand when you realize a human "only" has 5 to 6 million scent receptors in our noses, whereas dogs normally have 250 million scent receptors and whitetails have somewhere around 330 million receptors. 330 to 5 or 6? These facts alone will make us better understand what we are dealing with.

Here's a concept that is even harder to believe. Whereas individual identity is placed in the scrape through the scent of the tarsal glandular secretions, the physical condition and health of the particular buck is deciphered through the odor of the urine itself.

This has been biologically verified through our knowledge of an organ deep within a deer's nasal cavity known as the vomeronasal organ. This organ is rudimentary (undeveloped) in humans and well developed in deer, bear, coyotes, dogs, etc. The development of this organ is what differentiates the ability of one animal over another to be more successful at directional tracking. For example, the vomeronasal organ of a hound is more developed than some lesser breeds. The point being deer, both bucks and does utilize this gland at the scrape to choose the best mate. I will again use the similarities in studying domestic animals to coordinate my understanding of wildlife. When I do, I notice parallels that can be used to regulate everyday behavioral patterns. Did you ever wonder why, when two animals meet, be it dogs or deer, the first thing they do is smell each other. They'll either smell out their anal area or they'll touch noses. Why? It's simple, at least to them. They are using their vomeronasal organ to check on the health of the other individual. Remember when you were a kid people used to tell you that you could tell if your dog was healthy or feeling well by looking at his nose? If old Rover was feeling chipper, he'd have a cold, wet nose. If he was feeling down or had a fever his nose would be dry and warm.

We have all witnessed two deer touch noses. Don't let your mother tell you they are kissing. They are using their vomeronasal organ to determine the health of the other individual. This behavioral pattern is innate and simple to them, but it usually passes right over our complex, narrow-minded understanding.

After the scrape site has been accepted (primed) by the doe urinating in it, the buck is able to check the estrus state of the doe. He does this through the act called flehmen, in which he curls his upper lip pooling the scent of the doe in the front of his nasal cavity and often rolling his head from side to side absorbing every molecule of the does reproductive state into his vomeronasal organ. He's almost "tasting" her scent.

The doe, as we said, is testing both the physiological condition of the buck's health through her vomeronasal urinalysis and the personal identity of the buck through the odor of his tarsal secretions at the scrape.

To determine the buck's individual odor at the scrape is amazing enough to me, but the ability to determine the actual condition of the buck's health leaves me astonished. Her vomeronasal can actually determine the metabolic by-products of his urine. A buck in a heathy condition will be metabolizing body fat and will pass off this fat in his urine, whereas a buck in poor condition will be metabolizing muscle tissue (protein) and will consequently be emitting a different odor. Think about this for a minute. How many times have you been told when field-dressing a deer that has an excessive accumulation of fat inside the body cavity that it is a "fat/ healthy" deer? And how many times have you associated a lean; run-down animal with one that is in poor health? What I'm saying therefore, is a doe is able to pick the mate of her choice; the one that exhibits the best health, the best genetic dominance through his odor and thus ensures breeding with the most potentially strong and desirable sire within the herd to best/help perpetuation of the species.

The most important aspect behind all this biological mambo-jumbo is that all this takes place at or near the primary breeding areas. In other words, this, my friends, is where you want to spend your valuable time waiting for the party to start.

While we're on the function of scrapes let me mention the fact I have been asked if I prefer morning or evening scrapes? My answer is jokingly "yes." I've found not may guys tend to be "scrape hunters" per say. Most do not have the patience, similar to most don't have the patience to sit a single stand all-day... dark until dark, even when they know it's best during the rut. This is not necessarily a bad thing unless you have a very consistent, non-variable wind you can depend on. Because of heating and cooling air temps it's rare to have one wind stay directional all day.

Back to the original question, I find that most scrapes tend to get scent checked during the morning hours and actually worked (freshened) more so during the evening hours. And I'll tell you why. My theory is because deer tend to be more nocturnal, bedding more during the day, a big mature buck might tend to bed near a breeding scrape during the morning/daytime hours. It's very similar to a big, dominant boar black bear bedding down overseeing a bait barrel in the spring, which also happens to be the bear breeding season.

The subordinate bucks know a dominate buck might be bedded right there near the active breeding scrape, so they will tend to scent-check the scrape rather than risk getting confronted and chased off.

Whereas, in the evenings when a subordinate buck checks out a breeding scrape he feels more confident the dominant buck will more likely be on the prowl and is gone in anticipation for the nighttime upcoming orgy of rutting activities. And therefore, afternoon/evening scrape visitors are more likely to actively, actually work the scrape itself than morning visitors in my opinion.

But that's just my basic opinion, whereas things could get active at any time during the rut. If you have a good consistent positive wind and have the patience, you'll likely be better off staying on guard and letting the situation play out.

CHAPTER XX
NOT SO OBVIOUS DETAILS

A lot of preparation goes into my stand placements/locations. Because I intend to spend a lot of time there, I want it to be right. I've had comments on how much I "detail" my stand set-ups. I always assumed everyone did this but apparently not.

There are many pieces of the puzzle to consider. I want to touch on a few details to at least get guys to thinking. If nothing else, it will maybe make you consider some secondary options. I'm purposely going to try not to get into the big picture regarding land contours and/or structural positioning. This chapter will likely not be an easy read. It might even seem confusing and probable questions will arise. But the fact is it will make you a better hunter. Feel free to draw out little schematics if it will help you to understand.

Once in the right region you must pick the right tree. As I said many times before, I prefer a mediocre tree in a great position over a great looking tree in a mediocre spot. The fact of the matter is it's not often you find a great tree in a great location. And when you do it often already has a stand in it. Look elsewhere.

One of the most important aspects of a great stand location is an entrance/exit that will create as little disturbance as possible. Hunting an undisturbed area is fundamental. Be aware there is a normal rhythm in nature. Read that sentence again. When everything is copesetic there will be the normal "buzz". Background noises of birds, insects, frogs, etc. are both accepted and expected in the everyday norm. Temporary silence is a sign of disturbance. And all area wildlife will pick up on it. I learned this little tidbit from John Wayne. He was sitting around the campfire one night when his buddy (note... NOT his partner) said, "It's really quiet tonight", to which the Duke answered, "Yeah... TOO quiet Pilgrim!"

That's one of the reasons I'm an advocate of arriving on stand an hour early over a minute late in most situations. I want that buffer to lessen the adverse effects of my entry disturbance. Disturbing the "buzz" is also why I'm a big advocate of quietly remaining in position once the ambush has been established.

Changing stands, leaving for and/or returning from a lunch break, a potty break or whatever, will all disturb the normal buzz, thus costing you a half-hour before common "expected" noises return to normal. Game in the immediate area will absolutely, definitely pick up on this.

A low impact entrance/exit is vital. The smart hunter must consider sight, sound and scent in both his approach and departure. Let's use an example of each in illustration.

Often your stand placement might be just off the crest of a ridgeline. HUMAN nature is for old logging/skid roads to follow the crest of a ridge. It just makes sense for ease of travel for hunters and equipment. But it doesn't make sense for the deer. Although not always the case, deer will shy away from being sky-lined on a ridge top. They will normally tend to walk parallel to the crest, over the leeward side. It will depend on the angle of the terrain and visibility (density) but usually they will prefer being just far enough off to the side to keep their silhouette not obvious, yet passage where they can see downhill more so, or equal to being crested. They do this not through reasoning but instinctiveness. Think about it. It's just common sense when considering survival.

We as hunters must consider the same thing. When entering a stand site along a ridge line it's easy to walk the logging road along the top. This might be fine when it's dark (another advantage of stand approach before light). But when it's already light, or in the afternoon, you're usually better off picking your way in walking parallel to the crest.

If you do walk in on a logging road, I try to walk in the "tire track" of the downwind side. In other words, as an example, say the logging road is running north/south and the wind is coming from the west. You walk in the east tire track so the wind carries your residual ground scent off the road. This insures any deer that happens to be walking the logging road later will be less likely to smell your passage than if you entered on the upwind tire-track tainting the whole road. Adjunctive to this, if you use a scent-drag on approach you will notice it will benefit you even more so. Tie a scent-soaked rag or a Tampax off a four-foot switch and drag it (in the same example above) down the west tire track while you walk the east (downwind) track.

Because I'm a sweater I normally carry my extra coats/gear in a backpack. I prefer the great wool packs made by Bison Gear. When I get within a hundred yards or so of the stand I'll stop and put on my layered jacket, facemask, gloves, safety belt/harness. To ensure a quiet approach I sometimes pre-rake out steps to the stand. It's an obvious advantage to have your scent on final approach blowing away from the direction you think the deer will be coming/going.

I'll repeat this here also. For those of you who have hunted

Ladder stand before adding back cover

bears over a bait site, you will notice when multiple bears are hitting a bait, they will approach via specific footprints. This is a dominate/ subordinate situation. A subordinate bear knows if he is caught by a dominant bear on approach to the bait, he will get his butt kicked and it may be a fatal mistake. Therefore, if you look closely around the bait site, you'll see distinct,

Same stand after adding back cover

separate footprints/ pad marks that will insure the bear a more silent/safer approach. The subordinate will actually place his/her feet in the exact same footprint as a previous entrance/exit for a more covert (cushioned) approach. I like to do a similar thing when approaching my deer stand sites. I must clarify, I don't do this to all my stand locations, only specific ones, often dependent on the area bedding and visibility.

After the foliage drops in the fall, you'll have six inches of dry leaves covering the ground. Trying to walk through dry cornflakes quietly is a joke. If there is a cadence/rhythm to your gait it's almost impossible to keep your entrance/exit covert. Therefore, I'll use the "bear trick" to my advantage. I prefer to do this in the first week or so of November on a day that is not good hunting, i.e., a windy or rainy day. I use a garden rake or hoe to clear away the fallen leaves every couple feet for quiet foot placement. The result is especially important on quiet hunting days and/or within hearing or sight of a known bedding area. Of course, there are variables but I've often quietly slipped into a pre-set, pre-raked stand and take obvious advantage of the situation. You'll quietly climb into the stand and fifteen or twenty minutes later notice an ear twitch only a hundred yards away. Binoculars will confirm it's a bedded deer and you'll suddenly realize there would have been no way in hell you would have gotten to that point and into the stand unknowingly had you not pre-raked your approach.

After I rake my steps in, I take my trusty ratchet hand-pruners and clear away any major underbrush I might brush up against going in/out. This is not just for minimum scent retention but also for less noise of the understory brushing against the fabric of your pantlegs. This is all just common detailing that most people don't consider. Minor details are important.

I should note here I tend to weigh the odds accordingly. For example, on approach to a stand it's just smart hunting not to walk down or across game trails on entrance/exit. BUT if you think a circling approach will disturb too much area I'll opt for a more direct approach and actually cross the trail I'm hunting. For example, say you are hunting a main travel pattern running east/west. The stand is on the north side of the trail hunting a south wind. Your most likely approach might be to circle the stand and come in from the north. But if you do that you might be disturbing too much area and defeat your covert purpose. So, your best approach will be to walk in from the south where you have pre-raked and clipped a low impact entrance. When you hit the east/west trail you just step across the trail quickly leaving minimal ground scent and disturbance. The most import part of this is to ALWAYS, in situations like this, cross the main east/west trail right IN one of your shooting lanes. That way, if you should happen to leave any minor ground scent while crossing and any deer stops to check it out, at least he'll be standing broadside in one of your shooting lanes.

This is another situation for "bowling for bucks." On the way into the above scenario, I like to pick up a couple hedge apples (Osage oranges) with gloved hands. For those who are not familiar with them, they are the fruit of Osage trees. They are yellowish/green, about the size of a grapefruit, with a course texture on their outer surface. That outer surface is grooved in a squiggly pattern looking similar to a brain. To make it somewhat confusing, hedge apples and Osage oranges are the same thing when comparing apples to oranges. To this day, farmers still use the trees for fence posts because they take a long time to finally ground rot. Hence... the term "hedgerow". And of course, we all know the Osage wood is commonly used to make beautiful bows. Anyway, after climbing into my treestand, I'll take the hedge apple and run a bead of deer scent/lure around the fruit. By the way, those who don't have hedge apples growing in their hunting area can use a regular apple. It's just that the grooved

Ladder stand with artificial Christmas tree cover

outer surface of the hedge apple will accept the scent (especially a gel scent) better than the smooth surface of an eating apple. Also, be aware that some states who don't allow deer baiting could look at a scented eating apple negatively.

After running the scent around my hedge apple while in my

stand, I'll then throw/roll it across the trail right through one of my shooting lanes. Using the same previous scenario, if you approach the stand from the south with rubber boots, cross the east/west trail in a shooting lane, then roll the scent laden apple across the trail from north to south, the trap has been set. Think about it. The deer comes walking down the trail until it hits the residual scent laid down when the apple rolled across the trail. Because of his ability for directional tracking, he'll stop in the trail and look in the direction the scent-ball was rolled to/ laid out. It will offer you a broadside shot in a shooting lane, at a standing animal upwind of you, looking the opposite direction from you. It's perfect. And no audible directional bleat is needed to draw his attention to you. It's just smart hunting.

As mentioned above, I'll often play the odds. Bear with me on this. Even though it might appear a little confusing it's important stuff. Draw it out if that'll help. Let's use the same hypothetical set-up with an east/west trail, on the north side of the run, facing south with a south wind. Say it's more of a morning stand with the feeding area to the west and the bedding to the east. If it's a rut stand you might have deer movement east/west, 50/50. But if its pre-rut or post-rut 70% of the deer might be moving west to east in the morning and 70% of movement will be from east to west in the afternoon/evening. I like to play the odds in my favor. Therefore, I'll have two additional shooting lanes cut for multiple options.

Say you're looking straight south. If you want a broadside shot with the deer going west to east, I cross the trail a few yards to the east and roll the hedge apple from straight north to south in order to stop the deer broadside before he cuts my track. This way you are playing the 70% odds over the 30%. If you prefer a quartering away angled shot, I cut two additional shooting lanes. Again, you are facing straight south so I'll cut a shooting lane to the southeast for morning movement and another to the southwest for evening movement. If you prefer the quartering away angle you then cross the trail in the morning in your southeast shooting lane and roll your scent ball accordingly across the south lane. The exact opposite is used for the afternoon sit with entrance via the southwest lane. Clear as mud, right? Play the odds in your favor.

I also set up the shots by playing the odds with hinge-cuts and blockages. Before we get into hinge cuts let's talk about girdling. For those not familiar with girdling, it's a practice where someone cuts a circle all the way around the bark/trunk of an upright living tree. It can be done with an axe, hatchet, handsaw or chainsaw. This will cut off the lifeblood and kill the tree. It's a practice used to purposely kill the tree, which will eventually fall and open up the canopy, therefore allowing more sunlight to enter the surrounding grounds to stimulate thicker and better habitat/ understory densities. Yes, the tree will die, the problem is it will fall whatever the direction the wind happens to be blowing that particular day. You, basically have no control over it. Whereas, with hinge cutting you create the same effect but you're able to control the drop angle to your benefit. If you do any girdling or hinge cutting make sure you have total permission from the landowner and he/she understands what you are doing.

I much prefer hinge cutting so I am able to control the angles of drop. My definition of hinge cutting is cutting the upright tree straight across horizontally until it can be dropped/pushed over in the right direction. Because the tree is not girdled, nor cut all the way through, it hopefully continues to live. Yes, the tree will be horizontal to the ground but it should still be able to draw water and nutrients up from the soil. This opens the canopy allowing sunlight into the surrounding area, yet the still alive tree allows for continued leafing and promotes supplemental feed as well as ideal bedding cover with increased ground level densities. You get the benefits of both worlds. I usually hinge-cut trees that are six to eight inches in diameter and forty to fifty feet tall. Going easy with the saw you can control the horizontal cut until you can push the tree to the exact direction I want it to drop for my preferred benefit. Normally I make my cut just under four feet ground level. I want to use the hinge-cut as a blockage in order to nudge normal deer movement whichever direction I want. I prefer the cut at about four feet because I want the blockage high enough to shift their movement, yet low enough they'll not just duck under the obstruction.

Because I only hunt with a recurve bow, I prefer my shots to be at 12 to 15 yards. Not under 10 yards and not over 20 yards... but that's just me. Using the same directional example of a stand set-up as we did earlier, bear with me on this. The stand overlooks an east/west trail and you are facing south. But the trail is, let's say 25 yards from your stand and you want to shift the 70% W/E morning movement about twelve yards closer to you, offering a 13-yard shot. You pick a tree on the north side of the E/W trail and with your saw cutting four feet up, saw until you can swing the drop of the hinge-cut tree (the crown) to the southwest right across the main trail. This angle is very important. You want the brushy top of the tree (the crown) to make an obvious barrier to the west to east (70%) morning walking deer. If you drop the tree straight north to south the perpendicular angle might just force the deer to jump over the blockage. If you drop it to the southeast, it might angle him away from your stand defeating the purpose. Whereas dropping it at a SW angle will nudge the deer closer to your stand as he angles along the blockage. If you would have dropped the tree in a SE angle on a west to east moving deer, he may just swing wide and not give you the shot at all. The obstruction laying SW (in this case) will shift the normal movement and offer you a 13-yard shot rather than a 25-yard shot. After this shifting I then break out my hoe and rake a visual new trail down to bare dirt shifting around and back towards the original line of travel.

If you want to make sure the E/W (afternoon) movement is also nudged closer to your stand you need to hinge-cut a second tree about halfway up the southwest laying barricade. Drop it so the top(crown) faces southeast rather than southwest. Just make sure the base of the second tree is close enough to the first tree so an E/W traveling deer won't slip between the two trees and angle away from you, again defeating your purpose. If it will help you to understand please draw these little schematics as explained so you truly understand.

The same effect can be reached if you want to shift a deer's movement AWAY from your tree. I personally don't like really close shots at under ten yards. Therefore, you can create an angled blockage right under your tree in order to shift him from five yards to maybe twelve.

I apologize if this was a little hard to follow along. It's actually very simple but sometimes hard to explain. I fear some younger hunters today are not learning the woodsmanship skills to fully enjoy our sport. They are being taught all that is necessary is to sit over a food plot in a shooting house while playing a video game until a big buck appears. It's my opinion, spending time in the woods preparing for the hunt is half the fun. Not only is the father/daughter/son bonding beneficial in today's world but it will create valuable, life-long memories of earned and learned success.

I have mentored younger whitetail hunters for decades via the educational sessions I taught for fifteen years. As mentioned, some of this stuff is hard to follow unless you are actually shown. The bottom line is there will be a lot of satisfaction to your efforts. Not only will they watch a deer react exactly as you wanted and intended him to, but your efforts will hopefully shift his movement to a position where you almost can't miss the sucker-shot. And that itself will help hunting success rates tremendously.

> *"Time spent in the woods is both physically and mentally healthy"*

CHAPTER XXI
BEAR ESSENTIALS

I've missed my bear hunting the last few years. Over many decades I've hunted them in numerous states from New England to Montana, including five Canadian Provinces. I've bowhunted them in the high mountain huckleberry patches; walked many, many miles of old logging roads while they fed on the lush spring grasses and dandelion flowers. I've hunted them behind a pack of hounds once; spotted and stalked them from switchback roads through mountain clearcuts; sat old abandoned apple orchards; as well as pre-positioned bait sites. There's an obvious adrenalin rush when stalking to within ultra-close range of an impressive wild critter who could easily kill you. They have great ears, a nose second to none, and much better eyesight than most people give them credit for. You should feel proud no matter how you got within close range on purpose.

Although black bears are normally black, they are available in a wide variety of color phases. Additional to the most common black, I've taken them in about every color they come in from chocolate to cinnamon, auburn, golden red, blonde, root beer and a combination of any of the above colors. Plus, brown snouts; black snouts; large or small white chest blazes or no blaze at all, they are unique.

Similar to humans, I've seen a variety of physical structures, i.e., endomorphs, mesomorphs and ectomorphs. Everything from short and stocky to elongated, bigger boned bears and everything in between.

The bear I was forced to shoot because he got too friendly

Although I have killed two with rifles in my life, I normally just

Successful bear camp

enjoy close range hunting them with my recurve bows, taking literally dozens of them over the years. When it comes to bowhunting them, I am of the opinion they are very similar to big, mature whitetails in that for consistent close-range encounters you are usually better off letting them come to you. So, that usually means your highest probability for close-range bow shots will be hunting over bait.

Putting out bait isn't necessarily wrong. In certain parts of the country, it's the only feasible means of ever seeing a bear. An incoming bear will give you the necessary chance to study the animal, not to mention the ultra-close-range confrontations are very exciting. Although I certainly don't recommend it, I've actually touched a couple live bears in my wild and crazy younger days. From a bait you can usually see if they've got cubs. Sound biological management dictates not to shoot sows with cubs. I never have and never will. One biological research paper I read claimed once a cub reached thirty pounds it would likely survive on its own without the mother. But they are talking about being nutritionally weaned, etc. If the sow is killed the cubs are very vulnerable to other bears in the area. Older bears, especially boars, will intentionally try to kill the cubs through dominant traits. It's not a pretty scene.

Unfortunately, and also similar to some recent humans, its sometimes tough to determine the sex between males and females even for experienced hunters and even up close. It's hard to explain but it's similar to looking for differences between a male and female dog. The face of the female dog appears more feminine. It's more delicate, prettier than the masculine, blocky face of a handsome, male stud. But, through age structure facial appearances vary so it's sometimes tough. It's similar to comparing the face of a raghorn bull elk with that of a big, fully mature bull. The raghorn looks more like a cow elk with antlers. You get my drift.

Sometimes a big sow will be especially hard to tell from a nice boar. One thing to look for that is not common knowledge are "love bites." When a boar mounts a sow during the actual breeding process, he will often bite the sow on top of her back between the shoulder blades. That results in a pretty nasty, significant "love bite" that you can actually see from some distance. Anything anatomically visible there, whether some roughed up hide or an open wound will almost always be indicative it's a big sow. In fact, most bears you observe standing on their hind legs rubbing/ scratching their backs on an upright vertical tree are usually sows that are scratching the itchy, healing love bites. But... to confuse matters more so and show nothing is always, it sometimes is a bear (of either sex) trying to remove unwanted ticks. Look closely.

The bottom line is when sitting bait, it will let you study any bear, look for the sex of the individual and any young offspring present. As with most other species, when you see a really, really big bear there's no question about it... you'll know it, where as "nice ones" are deceiving at times. It's tough.

Similar to my whitetail hunting stand tactics, I put a lot more thought into a bait site for bears than most folks do. I don't just throw up a treestand for whitetails like I just don't just dump a bucket of donuts on the ground for bears.

First off, similar to whitetails, you need to pick the right spot. I prefer it to be near some water source. When spring bears first come out of hibernation, they biologically need to consume enough water to loosen/soften the mucosal plug that's been blocking their intestines during hibernation. Just before bears hibernate, they will consume dry vegetation, pine needles or even some of their own hair in order to form a mucosal plug that will keep them from defecating in the winter den. Water is necessary to initially pass this plug in the spring.

Study the terrain. I prefer a spot that is semi-open. Not too open, yet not too thick and tight. They like to be able to see the bait before approaching. Don't forget there is a dominant/subordinate pecking order around the bait site. And we're talking serious confrontations often with serious fights even to the death. Often, dominate bears will lay right next to the bait and "guard" it. Incoming bears, especially subordinates, will sneak in and/or circle to check the wind before entering. Others, rather than being sneaky, will purposely snap a branch so any bear already on the bait will audibly hear it and answer verbally by huffing that he's already there. You better get ready if you hear a significant distant branch break in the silence.

It's really interesting to watch. Some bears will sneak in on a direct approach to the bait. They'll take a few steps and lay down to listen. Then, advance a few more steps before laying down to listen some more. This is where you see specific, individual pad marks in the turf where incoming bears will purposely place their feet in previous pad marks/steps so as to better insure a silent approach.

Just as common as the direct approach, you'll have bears that circle the bait site, wind/ scent-checking everything before exposure to the bait.

Terrain wise, I also prefer a very slight grade uphill behind the bait site. Incoming animals prefer to approach a bait uphill. If you think about it, it's just common sense. If they approach from the uphill side any charging, dominant, bigger bear already on the bait will have a harder time running uphill than on the level. You have a better chance to get away when a fat guy is chasing you uphill.

So... a slight grade uphill from the bait; wind blowing at their backs so they can smell behind themselves and see in front; or sometimes come in directly downwind of the bait but still be able to see in the semi-open terrain; and don't forget, near some kind of water source close by.

Let me mention this before I forget. Once you've picked your bait site location, and before it's been hit I like to draw attention to the area through scent. If there is some kind of logging road you can drive a vehicle on, I like to use a scent drag leading up to or near the bait site. I prefer dragging from a vehicle rather than leaving human scent by walking it by foot. Drag a scent-soaked rag (oily tuna works well) or a piece of rotten meat. Drag it from two directions but always drag it towards the bait site. Don't forget bears are very capable of directional tracking/ scent trailing. Drag TOWARDS the bait site from different angles. This way any bears walking the logging roads will cut the aroma of the scent drags and directionally trail it right to your bait site. This little trick will open a bait site days earlier than if you fail to do this.

Let's build a scenario to compare strategies. There will obviously be some variables here but let's just consider generalities. Bear with me on this (no pun intended) as its educational stuff. Again, draw it out if it'll help to understand.

Say you have a predominate wind out of the north. We'll use north positioned as 12 o'clock in our example when viewed from above. Most guys will put their stand at about 6 o'clock and baits at 12 o'clock in our example. They are banking on most bears coming in upwind enough of their stand location at 6 o'clock. Some bears will, but a very high percentage will approach from upwind (from the north, then slowly circle around downwind in order to scent check what they might not be able to see visually. Therefore, if the hunter is positioned at the 6 o'clock location directly downwind of the bait, the bear will likely smell him, depending on the distance from the bait he's circling in relation to the stand itself and densities.

In our example above, I much prefer positioning my stand at a 3 o'clock location. Think about it, the bear approaches from uphill at the 12 o'clock angle. He doesn't see anything at the bait, so he slowly swings downwind, past the 9 o'clock position and downward to the 6 o'clock position where he can get directly downwind of the bait itself. So, he can smell anything behind him on approach; see anything below; then smell anything that happens to be waiting in ambush at the bait site on entering. Brilliant! ... except for one thing, I am positioned crosswind at the 3 o'clock position. He walks right into the bait with a head wind and false sense of security where the boogieman is waiting in ambush.

If you are baiting in the spring, this is also a great opportunity to add a little sow-in-heat sauce at the bait. If a circling bear gets downwind of the sow-in-heat he will be much more likely to follow the scent upwind rather than continuing to maybe circle. Smokey's deer lures also sell sow-in-heat lure.

Now let's talk about the bait site itself. I always preferred a metal 55 gal. drum with a lid bolted on. Wire/chain the barrel to a live tree. I also prefer a small 12"x12" cut out hole in the barrel where they have to work for the contents. If you happen to use grain/ oats as your primary bait, also have a few 3" diameter holes cut in the side of the barrel so they can roll it around dispensing grease-soaked grain or whatever. Oats soaked with added grease from the Colonel work well.

When opening a new site, the goal is to have the location known due to dissipating strong, inviting aromas. Starting with honey burns is a good idea. Put a couple inches of honey in an empty soup can and boil it on a portable burner/stove. I prefer using a small rack to hold the soup can above a can of Sterno. Bear in mind (no pun intended) if you use a nice heating unit or camp stove, the boiled-over contents will require some unnecessary clean-up later.

The honey will boil first, then go to a sweet, white smoke, then eventually burn down to a burnt/black smoke. Let 'er rip. I prefer to do any honey burns fairly early in the mornings rather than afternoons or evenings. That way there is still dew on the grasses and morning vegetation. The sweet smoke will stick to the moist dew-covered leaves allowing more residual smoke odor to stick so it can more easily be tracked to the source.

Once the bait had been initially hit you don't have to do anymore honey burns unless you want to. Bears prefer fresh bait. If you have a pile of fresh beef scraps alongside a pile of rancid, rotten, maggot infested meat, they'll go for the fresh stuff first every time. Rancid odors might attract them but fresh meats will feed them. Bears are actually opportunists so will hit whichever they prefer. I've had them not touch fresh fish (suckers) and hit soured meat laying right next to the fish. Go figure.

Once you have them coming to the fresh meat scraps and/or grains they'll like it. But now is the time to add the sugar/sweets. Once they've fed on the sweets they're hooked and will continue to return.

Next, the secret is to get multiple bears visiting your bait site. I'm going to share several secrets here that will help big time. One is to be sure to place some kind of strong, desired scent on the ground right in front of the bait barrel opening. You want a scent that is very odoriferous. Bacon grease is great, or a can of tuna fish packed in oil rather than water. Anise oil has a very strong aroma as well. The idea is for feeding bears to walk in the scent. The strong odors will stick to his pads, then, as he walks away from the bait, he'll leave a scent trail. Any additional bears in the area, on cutting the scent trail will back-track the scent right to the bait site. Once you have multiple bears hitting the bait the fun really starts. It's always entertaining to watch the interactions within the visiting personalities.

Remember, half of those bears will likely be sows. But also remember sows only reproduce every two years. Let me say this while I think of it. If you are trophy hunting for a big boar but are consistently seeing a bait site that has multiple sows with young cubs in tow... sorry but you should consider moving to a different area. Mature boars will intentionally try to kill young cubs. And the sows know that. Therefore, if a bait site has a big boar visiting regularly, the sow will take her cubs elsewhere in order to not expose her cubs to death.

At any rate, any sow in heat (only ones without young cubs) will attract the boars. So, returning to our set-up, now we have attractive/desired foods & sweets; scent; sex and nearby water all working for us. Now the idea is to keep them coming back and hanging around for longer times.

More little tricks. If you happen to have a screw-in treestep with a three-inch shank you won't need to pack a drill. Locate a downed log near your bait site. On top of the downed, horizontal log screw in your treestep and then remove it. Fill in the three-inch hole with either honey or peanut butter. They will literally spend hours trying to rip the log apart to try to get every last morsel.

Another tidbit I used to like to scatter around the bait site were chocolate chip morsels. Some people say, similar to dogs, chocolate chips are not good for bears. I don't know for sure but I really doubt a handful of chocolate morsels will hurt a 300 lb. bear, whereas a hundred jelly donuts at one sitting won't. Suit yourself. When I used to bait bears, I know those little brown morsels scattered around the understory would keep a bear looking for many hours.

Similarly, miniature marshmallows were another bruin favorite. A bag of those scattered through the leaves would keep bears around for more hours. I'm not sure if it was because they are white or the scent, but a single bear appeared to suck them up like a vacuum cleaner salesman.

Here's another little gem you likely never heard elsewhere. Pick yourself up the cheapest brand of uncooked bacon you can find. Maple/smoked works best though. Cut the whole package in half and take each separate piece of six-inch raw bacon and gently stretch it out lengthwise. You'll end up with a couple dozen strips of raw bacon. Not only is it odoriferous but both birds and bears can see it. Take each strip singly and wing it as high as you can into the surrounding trees near the bait site. The bears will try to climb for them but the added bonus will be the birds, including vocal ravens, crows, whiskey jacks and blue jays. All squawking their heads off trying to loosen and steal the bacon strips. All the noise will attract the attention of bears even upwind from long ranges. Remember, you heard it here first!

Another of my tricks is to place "satellite" baits additional to the main barrel. When I enter to rebait and/or sit a bait site, I'll carry in a 5-gallon bucket or a couple bread sacks of extra donuts or morsels. Say the barrel is fifteen yards and in this example at 12 o'clock from my stand. I place the satellite baits in a triangle location with the main barrel at the top of the triangle. Then, at about 8 o'clock at ten yards I'll add some satellite bait, usually sweets, plus an additional little pile at the 4 o'clock position also at around ten yards.

What this does is allow multiple bears the opportunity to feed simultaneously rather than one dominant bear keeping others off and risking them busting you while they wait their turn. You'll usually hear all kinds of vocalizations.

A beautiful Quebec bear

Another "while I think of it" tidbit that hardly anyone knows about. Often when sitting a bait in an area of heavy understory/vegetation you'll hear a "clicking" noise. No one seems to know what it is. When a bear is scent-checking a new area or bait site he will often do this. On scent checking, they inhale through their noses and exhale through their mouth. On inhalation, the bear's tongue is placed on the roof of the inside of the mouth. The tongue on the palate forms a seal so they can better smell the scent molecules they are testing. Then, when they exhale that breath, the "seal" of the tongue coming off the palate breaks and makes that clicking sound. The whole point is if you can't see a bear but can hear that clicking noise you had better get ready because it's another one right there!

More audible tidbits. If you should ever have a bear in a shootable location but not a good angle or position for the shot, you can make him move his position without spooking him off by hissing at him. A LOW hiss will cause a bear, especially a boar to stand up and move around slightly, often giving you the option of a better shooting angle. I would suggest you experiment with it on subordinate bears until you get the gist of it before you go trying it on a giant though.

And one last little tidbit you've probably not heard of before either, since we were speaking of hissing, this one is a lot of fun.

When you enter the bait site/stand carry in a can of pop. Shake her up really good and smear some peanut butter or bacon grease all over the can. Throw it on the ground near your bait site and have your camcorder handy. Mr. Bear will pick it up and eventually bite through the thin aluminum can spraying hissing pop-fizz all over his face. Since the hissing itself is a personal challenging noise in the bear world vocabulary, they really freak out and do back-flips, especially when it's right in their face. But... if it's a big one you better shoot him before he gets to the pop can though. And remember to always take the pop can out... don't litter.

CHAPTER XXII
PROPER VIRTUES

This chapter may seem boring, but I wanted to include it to get the readers thinking. As I have mentioned previously, I am of the opinion our youth of today are not being taught the vital woodsmanship skills of hunting. And it's our fault. Often "less is more." Stepping back to focus on plain, simple, yet proven successful methods are far better than the easier ways of some modern technology.

In yet another of my weird analogies, I've been noticing a lot of similarities between hunting and music. In a recent conversation with a friend, I mentioned I really do not care for the new kinds of music much. Yes, I'm showing my age, but there was something different about music fifty years ago. In all honesty, I can't say it was really that good either. There was just something different about Elvis, the Beatles/ British Invasion, Mo-Town, whatever. Think about it if you're old enough, five black dudes dressed in matching red and gold suits all singing "Doo-Wop-Do-Wop", while spinning around in sync. Elvis wore a rhinestone covered cape. Songs like, "Mrs. Brown You've Got a Lovely Daughter" or "Yellow Submarine" wouldn't make it past the four buzzers of "America's Got Talent, no less the X-Factor, American Idol, or The Voice.

I think a lot of musical attraction is/was memory by association. I recall a remote elk hunt myself and two friends went on back in the early '80s. Our tents were probably 20+ miles via winding gravel roads from the nearest hardtop. And we each carried 65-pound backpacks the last 3 to 5 miles depending on where we camped each time. On this one hunt my backpack happened to contain a small, mini tape recorder with a single cassette of "Willie Nelson's Greatest Hits." Each night after dinner we'd sit around the campfire swapping tales of that day while making plans for the following morning. Under the star-filled Montana sky, bright clear moonlight and crisp fresh air we could hear distant bull elk screaming their brains out...and softly playing in the background was old Willie singing, "Georgia", "Angels Flying Too Close To The Ground" and "Crazy." Even today, forty-plus years later, that music and those songs take me back to those wonderful years.

On another hunt we chased high-country mule deer on the Divide between Idaho and western Montana. That time, it happened to be, believe it or not, Helen Reddy. I honestly cannot say Helen Reddy, nor "I Am Woman", "You and Me Against the World", and "Angie Baby" were any of my favorite songs, but it just happened to be the only tape any of us had on that hunt. As I think back on that particular hunt, there were five of us in camp total. The sad fact remains my brother, Gene, and myself are the only two still living. With that knowledge, always make yourself great memories because nothing is forever. The fact is any time I happen to hear some of those old songs I am instantly transferred back to 1975 with refreshing memories of old lost friends and great hunts.

As stated, I prefer the old traditional, classic country music. Willie Nelson, George Jones, Merle Haggard and up to maybe George Strait. Some of the classic country hall of famers couldn't sing for beans in my opinion. You have to admit Johnny Cash and the rest of the Highway Men, often referred to as the Outlaws, did not have what one would call great singing voices. But... there was something special about them. Their style, the character in their voices and songs, something was unique that was hard to put a finger on. But we loved it. I honestly can't say I care for most of the new, modern country music comparatively. But that's just me.

I see a similar parallel when comparing traditional hunting to modern hunting. I hate to say it, but I also see a trend our great nation is going through to be very similar and getting worse by the day. To borrow an excellent quote I recently read, "Our country is going through cultural erosion rooted in ignorance, laziness and dependence. These are people who are out breeding us and out voting us." Notice its dependence rather than independence. So, it is with traditional versus modern technology. I personally am not against technology if it is used adjunctively to traditional skills and knowledge.

Look around at the present memberships of organizational hunting groups. The majority are comprised of older, bald, or white-headed geezers. Yes, I know it sounds funny but it's also scary. Where are all the younger guys? Where's the "new blood?" There are a few, but we need more, a lot more. I don't mean to preach here, but it's no one's fault but our own. In most organizations there are always a handful of individuals who carry the ball. It's the same guys shuffled around doing the same jobs year after year. The problem remains that those who are carrying the ball are all getting too old, too tired and too burnt out to maintain momentum. Please don't misunderstand me as I'm not saying the younger guys aren't doing a great job of promoting wisdom. I am saying there just are not enough of them. Again, I'm pointing a finger at ourselves because of apathy. We have let passion, enthusiasm, and excitement take a back seat. We are letting the romance die. We are trading love for lust. We are forced to decide exactly who is a do-gooder and who is a wannabe. The problem is some of the wannabes in hunting circles today do not possess the same amount of talent as other guys. The reason being, they developed their talents based on technology. Not to sound hypocritical, but the new wave of young hunters seems to duplicate the new wave of country singers. Maybe talent isn't the right word because I just stated above a lot of the older country artists didn't possess great voices. But they did, in fact, possess something special. Maybe its character or personality. Regardless, we must be extremely careful to maintain our focus on what is right, what is wrong and what is fair, remarkably similar to the direction our great country is apparently headed. The parallels are spooky, and we are faced with fear of the unknown. And I mean serious fear.

Please don't misunderstand me. I am very much in favor of the excellent movement to introduce young hunters into our midst via youth programs. Excellent! BUT I am also of the opinion these youngsters are not old enough yet to have the experiences necessary to make the correct decisions in the better interest of all involved. What I am saying is we need to additionally develop and nurture more of the thirty- to forty-year-old hunters to continue forward, to flip the ball to. Just like in our military, they must work their way up through the ranks. You don't go right from Lieutenant to General.

I also fear we don't have enough new hunting philosophers. We NEED the likes of great conservationists like Theodore Roosevelt, Aldo Leupold, John Muir, and George Bird Grinnell, etc. We need them to stir our thinking. We need them in order to form our own opinions and decisions for the future of hunting. There are too many whose opinions are based strictly on monetary gain. Maybe it's just me, but it also seems many of our more recent philosophies only arise when encouraged by overindulgence of alcohol. We need guys with wisdom to protect proper virtues. We as hunters, need leadership (along with our country) to uplift righteous, moral, and ethical principles of excellence. I fear human nature is leading most of us down the wrong pathway too often.

I'm a big fan of mentally planting a seed in hopes of generating enough interest and/or curiosity to kick someone off the couch in order to prove it to themself in the field. I'm a huge believer the more time a person spends in the woods the more reward, knowledge and gratification they will get in return. The old saying, "One candle lighting another won't diminish the flame" fits well here. Think things out and share your opinions with others. I believe the time to act for our future is not soon... but NOW. If we do not, we'll all be like Willie, singing, "Blue Eyes Crying in the Rain."

About a year ago I scrounged up an extra hundred bucks and went to the bank and bought myself a brand-new, crisp hundred-dollar bill. I started carrying it along with whatever other bills I had, for no other reason except the fact it made me feel good just having it if needed. I try not to break it unless absolutely necessary, and if I do, I replace it as soon as I can. You'd be surprised on how good that extra C-Note makes a person feel. Not only is it there if I need it, but I've stopped trying to hide my billfold each time I get some bills out to pay for something. I don't keep it to show off, I retain it solely because it makes me feel good knowing it's right there and its mine. It helps give me a good, positive attitude towards myself.

Attitude is a subject not often spoken of in hunting circles these days. Having a good attitude is part of feeling good

I'm a hunter and proud of it

regardless of if you're at work or play. I hunt because it makes me feel good all over. I'm a hunter and I'm proud of it. I don't hunt for any cheap thrill of killing an animal. I'm not on any ego trip either. I hunt because I love the entire process as a whole,

A death in the woods

every aspect of the endeavor. And no amount of convincing from anyone is going to change my mind. To love hunting is a basic step in the right direction. We must realize who we are and what we're doing in order to justify our motives in the field. Once we become "in tune" with our environment, then and only then do we gear ourselves with proper attitudes. Being in the woods carrying an instrument/weapon does something positive for my soul. It's not reliance by any means. Most of us don't rely on our weapons to carry us through the coming winters anymore. Nor is it a question of survival. But I get an indescribable good feeling in my bones on a crisp autumn morning as I get closer to everything beautiful that God has made. I'm more alive, closer to nature and closer to God, thank you.

Hunting isn't for everyone. Nor should it be. Because we are often purposely limiting our capabilities in the field, we are putting ourselves into a class of hunting that must lean towards a psychological approach. Reasoning is simple for some but becomes hard to grasp for others.

A lot of people might think I over-do it at times. They confuse the intensity with which I pursue my goals with the lack of intensity in which they pursue theirs. Hunting whitetails is a huge part of my existence. It's more than a pastime, it's part of my everyday lifestyle. That doesn't mean I get to go hunting every day. But it's on my mind, whether in preparation, contemplation or plain old daydreaming multiple times in a normal day, it's always there.

A person's nature is a direct reflection of the type of hunter he is. It's unquestionably hard for a person to remove himself from a high paced life geared to hyperactivity, then dive into the hunter's role as a predator, especially if one's nature is more like a raptor.

Accomplishing a goal makes anyone feel good but in the same respect we need to set attainable goals for ourselves. There's a definite difference between man's killer instinct (a term a lot of people don't want to talk about) and being downright blood thirsty. We need to accept that difference. False accusations toward intent have been drummed into our heads recently. We must stand our ground with everything pointing to the fact we are right and the antis are wrong.

I'm absolutely not blood-thirsty, nor am I out there for the kill itself. I hunt with intense purpose; to try to get the job done, so to speak. But each time I enter these ventures I go in knowing I am the disadvantaged and will very likely close the day empty handed, tired but completely satisfied. I have deep feelings and respect for the animals I hunt. I love them in a way no non-hunter could ever understand. I always have feelings for their welfare. A non-hunter cannot understand how any hunter would avoid hitting a deer with his vehicle yet try so hard to kill that same deer in the timber the next day. Only you and I know why we're out there. A lot of people just don't get it.

What is a trophy? For one person the definition likely will be very different than that of another. And this is the way it should be. Most of our memorable experiences will not be listed in any record books. We must admit the biological capabilities of our geographic hunting area and go from there. Trophy hunting is not for everyone. A trophy is in the eye of the beholder. It's a personal thing. If two big bucks were standing next to each other and one measured 169 inches, was wide and massive, ten points, but didn't make the minimum Boone and Crockett record book. But the deer right next to him, also with ten points, had longer tines, less width and less mass but measured over 170 inches because of symmetry. Even though they are both trophy bucks, I would take the first one because I prefer mass and width over spindly, longer symmetrical tines. But that's just me... that's my point... beauty is in the eye of the beholder. A run-of-the-mill buck from Minnesota could be a superb trophy from Florida or Rhode Island. Rightfully so. I once had a friend from Indiana phone me to tell me about his most recent buck. Not that it mattered but since I hadn't seen a photo I wanted to get an idea of its size. I asked him if it made the book. His answer was, "it made MY book." That statement sank home the reality of the situation. It meant a lot to him and that's all that really mattered.

By the same token we should all face up to the reality of our efforts. Not getting a particular buck last season may mean a monumental failure to some. But the positive side may spark the desire to try harder next year. We all have our off days or even off years. Last season I missed my chance at a phenomenal buck without even a shot taken. In doing so I fell short of my intended goal. But I also learned how to hunt this particular area more efficiently, to my advantage. So, in "failing", I learned something that will be helpful to me for the rest of my life... not a bad trade-off... especially if I was younger. Very often failures are blessings in disguise. Remember that!

Often, we don't necessarily need to learn as much as we need refinement of those skills we already possess. The plans I make while lying awake at midnight kindle a desire that will only elevate my satisfaction when and if I attain my goal. That's what hunting is all about. That's also what the antis are trying to make us feel guilty about.

Not to ruffle feathers, but it's also my opinion we as hunters must also stop hiding behind the "I eat everything I kill" philosophy. We cannot or must not continue to hide behind feeble excuses as to why we take to the hills. One major reason we are out there is for the personal/self-satisfaction of attaining a goal, as well as having fun enjoying ourselves. A famous quote is, "we kill in order to have hunted." That's it... period.

The quality of the average hunter has been decreasing steadily in my opinion. Only through the education of our forthcoming hunters will the future of hunting be sustained. I know I'll step on some toes here, but I get concerned when I drive down a country road and see literally dozens and dozens of shooting houses strategically placed around every food plot along the timber. Deer have accepted the uncertainty if these enclosures are manned or not. But the truth is, unless a big buck stays 100% nocturnal, he doesn't stand much of a chance. Yes,

No need to apologize for clean, honest hunting

sitting an enclosed shooting house is a nice way to be close to the kids, but please... please also take them into the woods and show them the practical applications of hunting.

Share the knowledge. I'm trying to do my part. Knowledge must flow freely to those youthful generations destined to follow in our footsteps. Sharing this information with children is of vital importance to their future. We have "broken trail" for their passage but we must trudge on through deeper snow. It is one way we can be certain the purity that has taken us decades and generations to develop will be properly regenerated for the future of our sport as well as for our sons and daughters.

For the past sixty some-odd years I have been the student. More recently I have tried to step up to the role of teacher. A transition such as this may cost us all a big buck or three, but the outcome will pay far more than it costs.

We need not apologize. Blood is not dirty. It's a part of life as well as a part of death of the game we take. Sure, we may put a damper on some of the more "colorful" game kill photos because a lot of people find bloody photos in poor taste. I agree. Try to show some respect. But the simple fact remains that bleeding is necessary in hunting. We don't need to regret its presence at the scene of our efforts. Blood is a direct result of our efforts and nothing more. Yes, I may wipe the blood from my hands before posing for a memory photo but I don't wipe them because they are dirty. I wipe them because the blood doesn't belong on my hands. I love the quote "The same person who takes offense of blood in a hunting photo will at the bat of an eye order a rare steak and slowly savor the red juices as they tantalize every tastebud in their hypocritical mouths!"

No, I'm not going to apologize for taking an animal's life in fair chase, so don't ask me to. Death must be considered a part of life. I pussyfoot around out there because I chose to be an omnivore. It's a deep-rooted quality that makes me feel good. And that about covers it... I like feeling good.

CHAPTER XXIII
HAPPY ANNIVERSARY

Sometimes I feel I'm cheating when I go out of my way to be sneaky. There's a small, 1.5-acre internal food plot surrounded by approximately 500 acres of mature timber I occasionally hunt. Although I have absolutely nothing against food plots whatsoever, the primary reason this one exists is to allow deer to feed evenings before they drop down into the cultivated crop fields farther west that are visible from a county road. The hidden plot just discourages drive-by shootings that might otherwise tempt passing vehicles. A lot of people don't believe this, but as of right now, if the truth be known, I have never killed a deer in a food plot in my life that I recall. As stated, I have nothing against them, I just prefer to ambush them to and from any plots themselves.

In this particular scenario there's an old farm two-track dropping down through the timber to the plot at the bottom of a ridge. It appears to be a no-brainer to access the bottom by just dropping down the road into the plot. This leads to the undeniable fact that in-the-field scouting time will teach you things you can't learn via just aerial maps or photos. Over the years I noticed after the foliage dropped, whenever I entered the food plot via the farm road, I would see white flags dancing across the flat and up the ridge on the other side across the plot. I could get away with entrance/exit there when there were leaves on the trees but not after fall foliage opened up the timbered view.

As you know, I've always been a big fan of hunting undisturbed deer. By doing so, we hunt them in their normal patterns rather than their altered, defensive movements. So, rather than risking any disturbance in the area, when I first top out the ridge, using the directional air currents to my advantage, I swing wide and quietly make my decent by slipping unseen down through the timbered ridge rather than walk the two-track. After dropping into the creek bed itself, I loop around and cross a weedy flat entering the stand via "the back door." It's literally hundreds of yards out of my way but well worth it. This is the way we must start thinking. When I point it out it's a very obvious no-brainer. But most guys are too lazy or do not even consider it in the first place. These are the little secrets that dictate your potential for success and what your hunt COULD produce. Literally, go way out of your way in order to hunt undisturbed deer. There will be that much of a difference.

So it was, on the afternoon of November 21, 2016. The name of the stand is Grand Junction because it sits where two old internal fences, a hedgerow and a bend in the creek bottom come together. To add to the positive mental side of things, I have personally seen at least four B&C class bucks from the stand over the years.

When I have to cross a main deer trail in order to get to my stand, I always make sure I do so in a shooting lane, so if any approaching deer happen to cut my track they will do so in a precise spot where I can take them if wanted.

The afternoon was beautiful, partly cloudy, 50 degrees and winds at 8 MPH out of the southeast. An hour into my sit, the first deer I saw was a great two-year-old up and comer non-typical. He had a really neat, twisted rack with several extra points. He's one of those you look at and dream what he'll turn into at full maturity.

Side Note: This buck was found dead four years later the results of an apparent long-range muzzleloader shot that was thought to have missed after the smoke cleared. He measured over 200 inches as a gross non-typical "buck of a lifetime."

He was about a hundred yards away from me on the flat across the dry creek bed. I filmed him as he dropped down into the creek and disappeared from my sight. Two minutes later and two hundred yards away I watched a bigger buck come off the food plot and also drop into the dry creek bed. He appeared to have decent mass and width with a honey-blonde colored 4x4 rack. It was obvious he'd made eye-contact with the young non-typical as the 4x4 was all puffed up with his ears laid back in an aggressive posture. Unfortunately for me, they were both now down over the bank and out of my sight. Five minutes later, up out of the creek two hundred yards away, came a 3x2 that I'd seen several other times previous.

Just then, movement caught my eye. On the flat at 150 yards was a really good buck, an absolute shooter for sure. He had pure white antlers and appeared to be a basic 5x4 with the body of a bull indicative of a fully mature stud. The direction he was headed would not bring him anywhere close to me so I decided to wheeze. He walked behind some slash and I couldn't see him anymore. I gave him another slap in the face with a second wheeze. I still couldn't see him and wondered if he could even hear my calling. Suddenly two does broke out of the dry creek bed with tails flying. I wasn't sure what was going on as I had a good steady wind and none of the bucks were chasing them.

For some unknown reason other than to assess the area, I looked behind me. Standing 40 yards directly downwind., opposite all the action, was another great buck. It struck me he'd apparently heard me wheeze, looked over and saw the movement of the does and was deciding what action to take. He was just standing there as I said a little prayer. Instantly, here he comes at a fast trot. He jumped the old fence five yards to my right. As soon as his hooves hit the ground on my side he broke into a slow run. It's kind of hard to explain but it was like his slow run was an announcement to the surrounding deer that, "I'm here... I'm the man... and I want in."

I hadn't shot a running deer for decades. When I was younger, I used to shoot them running all the time because I constantly practiced it. I was very good at it. I've probably killed well over a dozen deer running. But now with my bum arm I can't practice like I used to, so I've backed off.

Instincts took over. He was less than 10 yards. I drew and swung with his slow, steady gait. The instant I released I knew he was mine. The arrow disappeared right behind the shoulders broadside for a perfect double lung complete pass-through. Running about seventy yards he crossed the dry creek. As soon as he topped out, he stopped. I could see he was having a hard time standing. He was flicking his tail around wildly, which experience has taught me is a very good sign. Taking my eyes off him for literally one second, I looked back and he was gone. I wasn't sure if he stepped forward behind some brush or if he went down. It ended up he did both.

Making a long story short, as I approached him, I can't ever remember seeing a buck die in that position. He was flat on his back looking like a dog wanting a belly-rub. This buck meant a lot to me and will go down in my memory as one of my all-time favorites. As I was notching my deer tag it suddenly struck me, I happened to get him on the 57th anniversary of the day I killed

Happy Anniversary

What a beauty!

my very first deer ever. And a beauty he was. He has a basic 5x4 frame plus split brow tines on each side. He ended up measuring 161 2/8 inches with heavy bases of 6.5" on his right and 6.25" on his left with 25" main beams. Although I didn't weigh him, I'm sure he field-dressed well over 200 lbs. Looking at his teeth I'm almost certain he was 7.5 years old.

As he laid when I found him

The other reason this one was so special is because of my triple bypass, open heart surgery and subsequent cardiac rehab all that last summer. I easily could have missed the entire season… or worse. The fact is I could hardly draw a 35 lb. bow back on September 1, 2016. I borrowed an old 40 lb. recurve my brother had and left it strung and lying on the dining room table. Every time I'd walk by, I'd draw her back a couple times. Long story short, the day before our October 1st. opening day I put three arrows in a three-inch circle at 18 yards. with my 61-pound Tall Tines recurve. Even so, I promised myself not to shoot at anything over 15 yards. And I must brag... I kept my word when a potential Booner walked by me at 27-28 yards the last few days of October. I just didn't feel confident with the shot so I let him walk. I was admittedly disappointed but proud of myself.

Now, "the rest of the story." Two days later I was pulling SD cards from a couple trail cameras I still had out. Low and behold, there was a picture of my buck on a camera a half mile away. In all honesty I didn't recognize him at first because the time/date of the photo was after I'd already killed him. But on closer examination, the time/date obviously was off as it's definitely the same buck. I'll also fess up to the fact I really lucked out on the lighting and focus because the photo ended up winning a national trail camera photo contest that year. That's my story and I'm sticking to it

CHAPTER XXIV
STAND CHOICES

Recently I had a conversation regarding my stand choices and placements. Basically, I was asked how I decided which stand to hunt, when, etc. I tend to have a lot of stands. As I write this, I hunt a total of five farms totaling about 700 acres owned by four friends (one guy has two.) We manage the properties for quality hunting. In a nutshell, we keep them bowhunting only and try to take only fully mature bucks of 5.5 years or better. The landowners can allow whoever they want to hunt and whenever. But they have seen the results of our fine-tuned efforts. All we do is patrol the boundaries for trespassers, try to keep others honest and let the bucks grow. I also have to say we have ZERO tolerance on poaching. No excuses, no second chances, I don't care who it is they get fully prosecuted. The word has spread and they pretty much know we are dead serious about this and will get them.

I know the subject of trail cameras is somewhat controversial but one positive advantage is the fact new technologies will contact the landowner via satellite when someone is where they aren't supposed to be. I know a potential trespasser will think twice if he knows the farm has dozens of hidden trail cameras monitoring movement. Life is so much less stressful when everyone is honest.

I should mention right here, since my severe arm injury in 2001 (twelve screws and two titanium plates holding me together) I have gone almost exclusively to ladder stands. An interesting sidenote is the fact the first year after my brother killed his huge non-typical (233 inches) in 2004, we had a total of 33 (yes... thirty-three) treestands stolen from various private farms we hunted. Most of those were ladder stands and ALL were chained and padlocked to the trees. Frankly, it wasn't any kind of vengeance towards us or anyone, but more so a couple of young guys who were stealing everyone's treestands and selling them out of state for personal drug money. Having thirty-plus stands stolen is costly. The thing that bothered me the most was I went to the Van Buren County, Iowa sheriff's department to report the problem. I was absolutely floored when they told me they KNEW who was stealing them and their whole M/O. They said they were being sold out of state at various flea markets. Realizing that was a felony, I said "let's go." He said I couldn't prove they were mine anyway. I informed him I could since I had previously secretly marked them.

He said he was too busy. Let me get this straight, $3,000. worth of stolen goods that I could prove were mine; a couple felony convictions and known drug trafficking in small town U.S.A. with someone willing to press charges... and he said he "didn't have time for that stuff?" Don't tell me crime doesn't pay.

Over the years I've been really fortunate on some outstanding sales on treestands. One time a treestand company that just changed ownership and decided to drop one line of ladder stands, offered me great, brand-new ladder stands in the box for $20. each plus shipping. I bought twenty of them and wish I had bought a ton more.

My master plan is to have plenty of options available in choice trees in order to minimize hunting disturbances. When I was younger, I used to hang a stand and hunt it that same day. As mentioned earlier, because of my bum arm, I'm not supposed to hunt out of any stands I can't climb into with one arm. Therefore, I'm pretty much restricted to pre-set ladders.

Having multiple, well concealed, pre-set stands available to slide into with minimal entrance/exit pressure is just smart hunting. I have options for early season stands when the foliage is dense/thick; stands that are strictly observation stands, placed in order to learn movement patterns; rut hunting stands; all-day sit stands; late season stands for after the foliage drops; morning-only stands and afternoon/evening-only stands.

I also try to have multiple stand-sites for eight different wind directions on any one day. N/S/E/W/NE/SE/SW/NW. I often have stands that never get set the entire season, or maybe even for multiple years. I like options. It's just smart hunting so the local bucks have a harder time patterning me.

If by chance you are hunting public lands like I did for thirty years when I lived in northwest Montana, it maybe be foolish to leave your hung stands in place for long periods of time. In this case I used to pre-hang my stand before I hunted it. Actually, set it up. Clear out your shooting lanes; hang brush around the stand; clip out entrance/exit; etc. If you use screw-in tree steps back them out and stick a three-inch-long twig in the now vacant screw- hole so you can find the hole even in the dark without a light.

Get it all set to hunt and then pull the stand/ steps/ or rails and hide them close by. When the stand is primed and already detailed, a young skinny guy can slip in and set it up in relative quietness even on public grounds.

I like to "field-test" new stands. I will often set each new stand a couple mornings and a couple evenings to determine if

Add some Christmas garlands and leafy branches and we are done

they need any tweaking. For example, one new stand for this upcoming year has already been put up, taken down, shifted and/or moved a total of five times to three different trees, all within 25 yards of its original placement. The problems were the shape of the tree trunk (angle); branches creating potential problems for drawing bows/ hitting bow limbs, trying to take advantage of cover but not being too high or too low in the tree; being able to see but not be seen; sun angles at different times of day for me and against me; being sky lined, etc. Once you get it right you end up knowing it's the best it can be. And this will give you a more positive mental attitude, knowing it's the best. That positive attitude will lead to patience. I'm a huge believer of preferring a decent/good tree in a great location over a great looking tree in a mediocre location.

I should also mention when we first put up a new stand, we often put a trail camera near the epicenter of activity to monitor what's in the area for a week or so. I don't depend much on mental recall anymore. We tend to name our stands, which makes it easier to keep track of them when you have a bunch. If you don't name them, just number them. It's just easier/cooler to say, I'm going to "the Gut pile" than saying "I'm going to #17. I list my stand locations every year before the season. I keep separate charts for AM and PM stands. And I list stands on each chart for eight different wind directions so I have options all the way around.

I use a weather station on my computer. There's lots of good ones. But make sure you have one that listed HOURLY wind directions. That's an absolute must. Every evening before I go to bed, I check the hourly wind predictions for the next day. That way I fall asleep dreaming about my potential plans. The next morning when I first get up, I check the computer weather again. If you don't have a computer, you can get a cheap weather radio at Wal-Mart or Radio Shack.

Play the percentages. When I used to live in NW Montana the weather guys had a tough time with the predictions. They had to deal with the Continental Divide and some patterns coming in from the Pacific Northwest and others down out of Canada. Now, living in Iowa, the mid-west weather guys are scary accurate. You can plan your hunt and hunt your plan.

Say the weather prediction is for the morning winds coming out of the southwest and switching from the Northwest at 1PM. I go to my charts and look at my stand options for those two winds. Say for example I have nine stands listed for morning SW winds. I look at those nine options and know I have sat four of them in the last several days. I'll therefore pick another that is fresh and hasn't been hunted recently. I've already predetermined they are all good stands.

Then, knowing the winds are predicted to switch from SW to NW at about 1 PM, I'll go to my NW list of afternoon stands and plan my day accordingly. Like I said, plan your hunt and hunt your plan. It's just smart hunting.

Every piece of property has "sweet spots" with more game activity. ALL of my stand locations are dictated by the land contours. In other words, I've selected my locations dependent on terrain features and try to only hunt them with dependable wind directions. If you don't, you're doing nothing but educating the deer and making it tougher on yourself.

A recent afternoon hunt is a good example. I chose a stand that was best for a SW wind. The weather was warm and the days sun had dried the leaves on the ground to loud crispy critters. There was little to no wind, just a very slight breeze of maybe two or three miles per hour. After I got all set up and ready to go, I again checked what minimal wind I had. To my shock it was now coming from the NE. It had done a complete 180. Because it was so minimal, I decided to give it a half hour to see if it'd stabilize as predicted from the SW. In the first half-hour I got busted by three separate single does. Time to abort boys and girls!

I tried sneaking out the best I could but then decided my second option stand was in the open hardwood timber. Since the deer were heavily eating acorns, I'd be running late and both loud and visible on entry. No way. I decided to wrap it up rather than educate them to my presence. I really hated to do it but opted to not risk educating them. What's a girl to do?

Some hotspots are so good we need to have two stands only 25 yards apart in order to cover opposite wind directions. On the other side of the coin, we also keep areas with NO stands at all in order to create a sanctuary of safety for the deer.

Basically, I just play the odds. I pick and choose my best options from projected winds from the lists in order to keep the hunting pressure minimal. Always remember one of our biggest secrets is to try to hunt undisturbed deer. It's always money in the bank.

"Always have a positive mind-frame. Use common sense and reasoning"

CHAPTER XXV
STILL HUNTING

The term still-hunting is a rather gray area for me. Personally, I'm not sure if people don't really understand what it is, or they don't generally have the patience and therefore don't do it right. It's a frame of mind. What most people consider still-hunting is not what I consider still-hunting.

Some hunters just generally "go for a walk in the woods" and say they were still hunting. They might have been to a degree but there's a lot more to it than that. By my definition, still-hunting is simply a mobile stand hunter. If you're walking more than you're standing still in any one time period, you're not still-hunting in my opinion.

As I said above, it's a state of mind. When all is said and done, it's probably one of the best ways to become "one with nature." It stirs our predatory instincts and yet it soothes us into a calming disposition/mood as life unfolds around us. Quite likely, it may be the fact our slowed down pace allows us the time to absorb our surroundings. In fact, it often overrides the feeling of wanting to kill.

Most people are geared too hyper to be good still-hunters. It's not really their fault. It's mostly the rigors and hustle of everyday living that have us going through our routines at a much faster pace than we psychologically should be when hunting this stealthy method.

When we leave home, hunting camp or wherever in the morning, most of us tend to be in a rush to get where we're going too quickly. We're geared too high. We go to the area in fourth gear, drop down to third when we get there, and usually hunt in second gear. Some, a very few individuals, hunt in first gear. I'm not even going to give you that. I'm stating you should still-hunt completely "shut down", then ease forward locked in low-range first gear, then shut down again.

One very successful old still-hunter I once met told me one of his "secrets" to success. He was also of the opinion that still-hunting was a state of mind. His personal philosophy to success was to reverse the roles. He said he psychologically became the hunted rather than the hunter.

He said he'd go into the general area he wanted to hunt at a normal pace and then lay down on the ground, close his eyes and listen. He said if you listen long enough sooner or later you'll hear something. It may be a squirrel cutting or a branch breaking or a jay scolding... whatever. The point is that listening period gears him down psychologically. Then, when he hears the noise, he imagines "someone" is after him making himself move at the utmost of silence/ caution or else he will get caught. Yes, it's a mind game but reversing the role from hunter to hunted works well for him.

Before we get into methods of actually still-hunting, I think we should take into consideration the conditions that not only dictate the success or failure but determine whether you should be hunting in this way, on any particular day in the first place.

It's absolutely imperative conditions must be perfect. Still-hunting is much more conducive to rifle hunting than bowhunting. Although it can be done with the bow, especially during the peak of the rut when they're chasing and might just run into you. The whole concept is to see the animal before he sees you, slip within range, or let him come closer, and execute your shot. Unfortunately, this is not always the case whereas the animal detects the hunter and takes off. If hunting with the bow the situation is usually over when game is jumped. Whereas with a gun, even though the animal is disturbed, the hunter still has the capabilities to reach out and "reduce him to possession."

There's a huge difference between conditions being perfect and being acceptable. I much prefer an overcast day rather than sunshine. I pretty much hate sunshine anyway. My wife says sunshine will put you in a better "sunny" mood. Personally, I'm in a better mood when it's cloudy because the hunting is better. Get it?? Better hunting... better mood. Hunting is always better on a cloudy, dreary day. You know why hunting is always better in the early morning, evening? It's more like a cloudy day. If the sun is shining bright it's usually too hot, game is holed up, visibility is poor because of excessive brightness versus shadows. I'm always squinting, sweating. Etc. Hell... sunshine will even burn you and give you cancer. As a hunter, I can't say I love sunshine and you can quote me on that.

My apologies for that rant but I prefer a cloudy, overcast day to slip around. I like it even more if there's a slow drizzle occurring. I don't mean a downpour or soaker rain; I mean a slight drizzle. My favorite is when it's like a heavy mist in the air. Everything is soaked thereby keeping my noise to a minimum, and still, I have some minimal dripping in the background to help cover any mistakes I happen to make.

Same with wind conditions. A lot of guys say they prefer no wind so they can hear. I prefer a slow, steady breeze of a couple MPH. If the woods are wet you aren't going to hear much anyway. A deer walking on wet leaves with pointed hooves isn't going to leave much to listen to. I'd rather have a slight, steady breeze that is dependable for my movement. Having it directionally consistent is the most important factor. A variable breeze is terrible to deal with so don't even consider still-hunting in those conditions. When you have no wind at all there are still some slight shifts one way and then another, ups and downs of drifting eddies before, and if, it settles into any specific direction long enough to depend on. Any individual who is properly still-hunting (slip-hunting) is covering way too little ground and remains motionless in one particular area for too long to put up with any mild or variable wind shifts whatsoever. Forget it... it ain't gonna work and you'll just be disturbing the area and educating the deer. But the good news is quite frankly, days with absolutely NO wind are extremely rare.

I always try to still-hunt with the breeze in my face, quartering into the wind or at the very least a crosswind. Different individuals may have different preferences that may depend on the immediate area, terrain and densities. For example, it's very possible to have close range encounters in very windy conditions. One example is within a standing, unharvested cornfield. Another is on river bottom flats in vast areas of wild rose bushes. In mid-October we often find the deer feeding readily on rose hips. On extremely windy days all you'll see their racks rolling back and forth, "floating" above the wild rose bushes. My guess is they are too busy separating the rose hips from the stickers because if you take your time you can get right up on them.

Over the years I've also had some close encounters still-hunting on dark, misty, wet afternoons in old grown-over or abandoned apple orchards. I think the moist air carries the aroma of sweet, fermenting apples down through the timber so the deer can't wait for nocturnal feeding. I've literally busted them out of an old apple orchard and half an hour later they'll be back.

Obviously, we can't control the still-hunting conditions but we can control other factors that improve the conditions. Take camouflage for example. Try to make your colors match the surroundings. Dark green camo tends to stand out as a dark blob against a lot of backgrounds. In the same respect, a lighter "desert" camo pattern will not work as well when hunting in second growth softwoods. In some areas it is possible to still-hunt in softwood terrain but usually the density of the cover will limit your visibility making hardwoods or semi-open terrain more conducive to slip-hunting. Color-wise I've always preferred shades of gray and brown over darker shades of greens and black.

Other than winding you, the way most deer will nail you will be through your movement. This dictates total camouflage in my opinion. And I mean total camo and I'm not referring to specific camo patterns. Any dull or broken camo pattern whose color schemes blend into the surrounding will work well. This also includes snow camouflage. When snow is on the ground I'm a firm believer basic white camo with a few darker streaks/branches here and there will be a much better color scheme than any of the darker, regular patterns. Deer aren't used to seeing anything white chasing them and don't as yet associate a white pattern with danger.

As important as any one thing, it is vital to still-hunt with a facemask and gloves. I can't stress this too much. As with deer-drives, you are at ground level and therefore eye level. Other than actual mobile movement to and from your hunting area, donning a facemask when at ground level will increase your success dramatically. Yeah, I know it's a pain in the neck, but your chances of being seen and/or detected at eye level will be decreased greatly if you don't show them a white face floating down through the timber.

Clothing material is very important. You have to have an outer surface that is soft and quiet. Chamois is okay as long as it's dry. Once chamois is wet, be it from the morning dew or precipitation, it tends to send out a mildly offensive rustle that impedes my hearing. They may not be able to detect the noise of wet chamois from any appreciable distance but I don't like noise myself. I much prefer wool, polar fleece or even sweatshirt-type fabrics. Yes, it will pick up burrs but I consider it a good trade-off. It's quiet. And like my friend Mike Prescott says, "If you ain't in the cling-ons… You ain't in the bucks!"

Footwear, or lack of it, is probably another one of the most important dividing factors in successful still-hunters. After hunting barefoot with some Hawaiians one of my friends gave up shoes in April and went barefoot through September. Going without any shoes for six months really toughens up your feet. Yes, they get calloused and hard but they are superbly quiet. Unfortunately, living in the northern hemisphere, dealing with seasonal variations (snow) makes it unreasonable for us to consider doing this. When the Hawaiians feet crack and split, or they get cut they eventually heal up where the scar tissue makes them all the more tough. When we get a cut on our bare feet, by the time it heals the snow is flying and the season is over. You get the drift (no pun intended). Besides, I'd get tired of all the "No Shoes; No Shirt; No Service" signs.

Another thing to consider is NEVER go bare footed in terrain that has black or honey locust thorns and/or cactus. I've had locust thorns penetrate a heavy, lug-sole boot as well as a heavy-duty new ATV tire. Not to mention the locust thorns are very toxic and penetration will often get infected to include blood poisoning. Sand, pebbles, rocks, etc. may be fine but stay clear of the mid-western river and creek bottoms with locust flats.

Being able to feel the ground through a thin, flexible sole are important when stalking. When a person normally just walks slowly, they place the heel down first, then roll forward onto the ball of the foot. This normal walking pattern/gait does not adapt well to still-hunting. Whereas if the ball of the foot is planted first, the abnormal step will psychologically make you aware you are specifically placing your foot.

Because the ball of the foot is wider than the heel, you'll have better balance when planting the ball first. If you feel a twig underfoot, you can raise up the forward foot and reset it before the weight is distributed to it. Always have the weight firmly planted on the rear foot until the ball and heel of the forward foot are set firmly and quietly. Being conscious of planting the feet like this will automatically slow down your pace. But always remember to pay just as much attention to your surroundings as you do to your foot placement.

Because you are moving at such a slow pace you are able to pick out the route that best suits your approach into or through the immediate area. Keep below any ridgelines so as not to skyline yourself. Also try to keep towards the shadows/shade as much as possible. Move slowly from the shadow of one tree to the shadow of the next. Taking any wind consideration as a priority, try to keep the sun at your back. It will definitely help if the animal is somewhat blinded by the morning or evening sun in their eyes.

Even though you try to keep the sun to your advantage, it's best to still hunt with some kind of cap with a bill to block out any backlighting. Especially in low light morning and evening conditions you'll notice if you try hunting without a bill on your hat you'll lose a lot of detail to backlighting.

Always use any available ground cover or brush to conceal your movements. Move up to a piece of cover and stand behind it until you feel the coast is clear. Then slide around to the front side of the cover remaining motionless to use your new background as a cover. Remember, any lower brush of the understory will help minimize your leg movements as well, so bear that in mind.

Scrutinize everything while looking for detail and color but most of all look for movement. Movement on the animal's part will be what your eye picks up first. Train yourself to look in segments rather than scanning. This will definitely help your eye on picking up movement.

Most guys tend to look too high. You'll want to scrutinize your efforts at the thirty-inch height. In thick cover or in an area that has an overstory or low browse line, squat right down and look under the normal human eye level. Remember prey species will not pick up vertical movement as easily as horizontal movement. You'll be surprised at how much farther you'll be able to see in areas by squatting down. This will really help you. Man's average eye level is probably five or five and a half feet, while a deer's is only maybe three feet. If you don't squat down they are going to get you before you get them. But always bear in mind your movements should always be in slow-motion. The advantages of bending or squatting far outweigh the disadvantages of excessive movement.

If you think you hear something, stop and cup your hands behind your ears. Doing this will seemingly increase the volume three-fold. Don't laugh. Why do you think deer ears are cupped? Not to mention they can rotate those cups and focus their hearing potential behind themselves as well. If you don't think it makes that much difference, try this little experiment. Sit behind the wheel of your car with the radio playing normally. Then cup a hand behind each ear. It sounds like someone doubled or tripled the volume.

Watch your breath when you are still hunting on a frosty/sunny morning. First of all, if you're getting winded (out of breath) while still-hunting you're moving way too fast. A good still-hunter should not get out of breath while climbing the highest/steepest hills. He should be moving way too slowly to get out of breath. The original point I was trying to stress is the fact if your breath is producing visible breath vapors, deer can detect those breath vapors at fairly long ranges, especially in the cold morning sunlight. That's just another reason to try to keep to the shadows. Breathe through your nostrils. That will cut the noticeable vapors almost in half.

I remember one great stalk I pulled off maybe forty years ago while still-hunting whitetails on an island in the middle of the Yellowstone River of southeastern Montana. I used to love to slip these islands that I could wade to because they got little to no hunting pressure from anyone else. The sandy soil of the river bottoms made for some exceptionally quiet walking. When slip-hunting in sandy soil if there are dead/dry leaves laying on top of the sand it's easy to use your bow tip or a willow "switch" to flip any debris aside from where you want to place your next step. I swear island deer seem to be less aware and more relaxed, I assume because they are hardly ever harassed out there on the islands surrounded by water.

This one morning I looked up after my eye caught a huge rack from a giant typical whitetail who was bedded down behind a pile of driftwood. My plan was to slip within good bow range and just wait him out until he stood up, even if it took all day. He was worth it. I literally had to either squat down or clear myself an open spot with my bow tip to place my next step. Tension was high as I inched forward and his giant rack became more enormous with each step. I was sure I was about to either kill a B&C buck with a bow in his bed or there would be an explosion of muscular power as the giant leaped from his security bed. Even if that would happen, I was now close enough where I could snap-shoot an arrow through his lungs before his front hooves hit the ground on his initial lunge.

But the bound never came. When everything finally came into focus within the branches of the surrounding driftwood, I felt like an idiot when I realized it was not a buck I was stalking after all. It was a giant shed antler that had been washed atop the pile of driftwood during the previous spring floods. It had just coincidentally settled perfectly upright into a position that had the appearance of a big buck bedded behind the driftwood.

I saved that 5-point shed antler for twenty-five years to remind me of the experience. Unfortunately, I lost it in a storage shed fire in '99. Until that day it was one of the prettiest single shed antlers I've ever seen. It had graceful, flowing lines on each long tine and if given a 20 inch inside spread to a match he would have measured in the mid- 170s.

As I said earlier, when it comes to producing real trophies, still-hunting is more conducive to rifle hunting than bowhunting. No matter how careful and sneaky you might think you are, a good, mature buck will usually catch you off guard before you catch him. If you've done everything else right, he may spook and run out a short way, stopping long enough to make a decision. This short length of time is often long enough for an alert rifle hunter to drop the deer on the spot. But alas, the poor bowhunter usually stands there with the frustration of the deer out of range and the entire area spooked on red alert. And that's usually the majority of the time. But when everything goes just right... that one time in dozens when all the cards fall just the way you want them to... that's when the challenge and thrill of the experience equals or exceeds most any one-on-one hunting experience you'll ever come up against.

CHAPTER XXVI
COMING FULL BOAR

My brother Gene and I used to organize bow hunts for feral hogs in Texas. We did it off and on for probably twenty-five years. Texas used to sell a five-day non-resident license so we structured the hunts to be Mondays through Fridays normally. Guys (and some gals) would drive in from all over the country the weekend before their scheduled hunt, then drive home the next weekend. In 2011, we had five one-week hunts alternating between three separate locations starting in early February through mid-March.

Most of the hunts included free primitive camping. A few included a camp or bunkhouse option depending on availability. And most we would BYO food so each group could eat at their own time preferences. Because we limited our hunts to between fifteen and 25 bowhunters, the huntable areas had to be fairly large. Several of the ranches were over fifty thousand acres. Rather than hunting the same acres two weeks in a row, we'd divide the ranch in half allowing all the hunters fresh acreage if at all possible. Over the many years we tried to learn from our mistakes. All in all, the hunts were very well received; very reasonably priced because of the free camping and BYO food; and a lot more fun than shoveling snow in the northern states. Not to mention feral hogs are fine table fare if cared for properly.

Obviously, we have no control over the weather. Over the years it was necessary to roll with floods, mud, drought, late-season snows, gale-force winds up to 70 MPG, dust storms, etc. For example, one morning that year we awoke to three inches

Off Season Fun

of fresh snow and temps at 6 degrees, with a windchill factor of six below zero. Three days later it was 91 degrees. The hunters were great about it all and continued to hunt hard despite the conditions.

On our first hunt in 2011 a total of only thirteen bowhunters killed a total of 24 hogs in just 3 ½ days of hunting because of poor access and nasty weather, etc. Then, some other years the weather is gorgeous like it's supposed to be, so you never know. I remember one year I killed eight hogs myself in one day so it was a "target rich environment" and a ton of fun.

Friday, March 11, 2011, was the last day of our fifth hunt. Although we share a common campsite with all the hunters, Gene and I hunt also. Because the ranches are huge, Gene and I usually pick a smaller area out of the way in order to hunt for ourselves. On Thursday (March 10th) my brother and I offered to share some of our spots with the other hunters for the last day grand finale.

A "mature" bowhunter from Wisconsin named Bernie Finch was 73(?) years old and had a big boar on his bucket list for years. Gene put Bernie into one of my treestands while I put two other hunters into two of our other spots. I'm pleased to say the initial guy got his very first bow kill with traditional equipment that evening; and the second guy also got covered up with hogs.

Bernie had a big black boar come in late in the evening. He made what appeared to be a good shot but hit the back part of the shield and didn't get complete penetration. The boar only ran off a little way and tipped over. Bernie could see the arrow still moving occasionally but it was almost dark so he wisely backed out. A half-hour later Gene came to pick him up and they blood trailed until they saw the boar. Bernie missed a finishing shot and the boar ran off. They decided to back out until morning... the last day.

Friday morning Gene, Bernie and I took up the trail. Bernie was on my left and Gene on my right. I had just spotted the hog

Another big boar

myself when Bernie shot. I quickly followed up with another arrow as the hog ran away. I ran after the boar to keep him in sight and to try to finish him as quickly as possible. I couldn't tell whose arrows hit where or if at all. Suddenly the pig spun around, saw me and charged. At a distance of about fifteen feet, he was coming full boar (no pun intended). And he meant business. This was no false charge. I saw he dropped his head just before he charged. I came to full draw and sunk a great shot where his neck and shoulder meet. Yes, it was a frontal shot, but that was my best option. The shot sunk deep through his chest cutting the carotid artery, angled downward, took out the top of his heart and exited behind his right elbow. It was perfect shot placement but unfortunately momentum kept him coming.

Here lies a bit of information that may be vitally important someday and hardly anyone knows about. If you're ever faced with a charging critter and you've just shot your arrow, you have no time to reload. Without hesitation throw your bow in the critter's face. I call it "the sacrificial limb" (the bow limb... get it? Sorry!) Seriously, the critter will often fight with the bow thrown in his face, giving you just enough time for a clean get away.

So, with no time to reload, I threw my new Tall Tines recurve in his face. As I turned to run, there was a rather small, 6-inch diameter mesquite tree I shinnied up. I found it interesting when I was in high school I held my high school record for the rope climb (Class of '62 RULZ) but I could barely make it up a few feet at age 67. At any rate, the arrows finally took effect and he died right at the base of my tree. Let me put it this way, when I came down out of the tree I almost stepped on my bow tip... but he was dead. All my brother said was, "aw man... that would have made great video!"

He was a nice mature black boar that later weighed in at 194 lbs. with nice tusks, so Bernie's dream came true. I have to admit I did pretty good on that one but the next one I didn't do so hot on.

Later that afternoon I was heading into an area five miles

away (a 42,000-acre ranch) where I had a ladder stand next to a remote farm pond. Gene dropped me off and said he'd be back at dark. As I approached, I saw a group of two mature sows with seven or eight piglets drinking at the pond. After scrutinizing them in my binoculars I decided the one was a dry sow and the other nursing the piglets. The wind was fine so I dropped down below the pond levy and just barely reached a bent over tree where I'd killed another hog three weeks before. Here they came, rounding the end of the water. I again noticed the calico sow was lactating but the large black sow was apparently dry. She walked by me at about ten yards and I zipped a shaft through, right behind her shoulder. It was a complete pass-through and the entire shaft was soaked in blood.

I thought she'd go down before topping the ridge but the whole group made it over, even though she was lagging behind. Hmmm. Just to be on the safe side I gave it a half-hour and easily walked right along the blood trail. After topping out I noticed the bloodletting up somewhat but still no problem following her. Then, it started to get sparse.

It was pretty open terrain on top with just the occasional tree on a big prickly- pear cactus flat. Easing along I finally spotted her laying on her side. I assumed she was dead but per usual, just in case, I nocked an arrow and quietly approached downwind. When I got to about twenty yards she suddenly rolled up on her stomach, then looked over to her left and saw me. Still on her belly, she shifted to an angle facing me. That should have been my first red flag. There were two small trees between us about four or five inches in diameter. One was maybe ten feet from her and the other maybe fifteen feet. I shifted my approach angle so that each tree covered each of her eyes. Kind of hard to explain but my intention was to blindside her. I quietly advanced forward to finish her. When I got about forty feet away it appeared she was still watching me. Because of the poor shooting angle, I slowly stepped off to my right to try and get a shaft into her at a more lethal angle. I saw her move her feet into the starting blocks. That should have been my second red flag. Knowing she was ready to bolt I put another arrow into the only option I had. It hit just behind her shoulder and blew all the way through exiting just in front of the opposite back leg. She jumped up and took off away from me.

I'm purposely adding every minor detail here in hopes we can all benefit from my mistakes. When she ran off, I ran after her trying to keep her in sight (not running with an arrow on the string). Then I realized I was gaining on her. When any animal is wounded their tenacity is impressive but I wanted to finish the job as soon as possible. When I got to about fifteen yards I sunk another arrow behind her ribs quartering away. That did it. She spun around to face me. I quickly reloaded. Now she was facing me at about 30 feet. We had a big stand-off. Don't ever show a growling dog (or hog) you're afraid of them. I stood my ground basically because there were no trees nearby to climb. I started this ordeal so intended to finish it like a man. She just stood there at about 30 feet popping her teeth together. It was pretty intimidating but I was basically waiting for my previous arrows to drain her.

Then the inevitable happened. She dropped her head, just like the boar in the morning, and charged. For some idiotic reason I thought it would be a false charge so I stood my ground. When I finally came to the realization this was not a false charge, she was picking up momentum.

When these things happen to me I kind of go into "autopilot" and instincts take over. I'm no expert on this, but I think the mental subconscious mind kind of takes over and makes our memories somewhat foggy. I'm pretty sure we often react without thinking. But in this case, I recall thinking I've only got one shot so I better make it count. With no other options I tried to brain-shoot her at about five feet. The arrow hit pretty much right between her eyes but missed the brain cavity. It knocked her off her feet but she instantly got up and came for me. With no time to put another arrow on the string, I went for the old "throw the bow in their face" trick. I threw my beautiful Tall Tines recurve in her face and turned to run as I realized she was working my bow over. Just like in all bad dreams when some bad ass is chasing you and you fall down... well, dreams come true. I didn't run two strides when I tripped over something (maybe my own feet) falling face down right into a giant bed of prickly pear cactus.

Turning on my side I saw she was still taking her aggression out on my bow instead of me. Then she flipped it towards me with her snout. One time she flipped it aside and I kicked her in her face. Another time she threw it in my lap and I threw it right back into her face. I never actually got bit other than on my boots. The "bow in there face trick" vented her aggression and saved me for sure... remember that!

These next two parts I found interesting. One: even though I was rolling around in a bed off prickly pear cactus, I don't remember feeling the thousands of thorns sticking me like a thousand needles. I never felt a thing... right then. And the other thing: when I was laying on the ground with her standing over me I could feel she felt dominant and I was subordinate. But when I regained my feet, stood up and suddenly became taller than her, she started to back up. Then the thought struck me whether she was backing up to leave or just to get a running start for me.

Continuing to pop her jaws, I looked her right in the eyes, slowly took one step towards her and reached down for the tip of the lower limb of my bow. A quick glance told me it appeared fine, other than there was only two broadheads and a Judo-tip blunt in my still intact quiver. Getting the bow back in my hands gave me some confidence realizing I was somewhat in control again. I quickly nocked the next to last broadhead and sunk it into her chest. She moved off to about twenty feet and just stood there. Knowing I only had one broadhead left I figured I better save my last bullet just in case. Standing there waiting for her to die guilt overcame me and I thought I couldn't ask for a better finishing shot. I was about at half-draw on my last broadhead when she suddenly tipped over. WOW! Thank you Lord!

Standing there it was like someone suddenly turned the page. All of a sudden, I realized I was in a LOT of pain. Falling face down into the cactus bed, I looked at the palms of my hands. They were covered with literally hundreds of thorns. There were a lot of the longer two-inch needle thorns, but there were dozens of "bouquets" of smaller thorns in clusters all over my forearms, ribs, knees, thighs and shoulders. Not to mention my back, buttocks, hips, and legs.

In the heat of the battle when I grabbed the riser of my bow to take the last shot, I'd either broken off dozens of thorns or drove them in deeper. And these were those little darlings with barbed needles. Wonderful! Then, I remembered I had a little pair of field tweezers in my right front pant pocket. Digging into my pocket with a thorn infested hand really woke me up... Then

I also realized I'd lost my senior citizen reading glasses in the fight and I couldn't see up close to pull the thorns anyway. Plus, I noticed my hands were now really shaking, I supposed from the adrenalin rush. And my right arm was suddenly really hurting too. That was the arm I had twelve screws and two titanium plates in from a previous severe break ten years prior.

I stumbled my way back to where I originally shot from knowing I'd left a sweatshirt laying on the ground there. Both my t shirt and camo shirt were totally infested with thorns. So, I threw them in my pack and put the sweatshirt on.

I also knew I had to pull a ladder stand since it was our last day. So, I pulled the twelve-foot ladder, the trail camera, the rachet straps, safety belt, plus carried my bow 500 yards around the pond and up over the hill. When I finally reached the top, I looked back and there were five more hogs at the edge of the pond. I had a perfect wind and one used, but okay, arrow... so.... No way. Stick a fork in me... I was done.

It was about 6:45 PM now and there was still about 45 minutes left of prime time. Then I noticed I had a single bar on my cell phone. Gene had the truck and he was about four or five miles away. Knowing this was the last hour of the last day of five straight weeks of hog hunting I called him. I told him I got a hog and we could probably drive right to it but I had to kill it in hand-to-hand combat; fell in the cactus patch and was covered literally with thousands of thorns; I thought my right arm might be broken and I was totally dehydrated and as thirsty as I'd ever been in my entire life.

I'll quote him... he said, "Are you bleeding? I said, "no... not really bleeding." He says, "If you ain't bleeding... you ain't needin'... cowboy up... I'll be there after dark." Then he hung up.

The one that got me. Notice the broadhead hole low between the eyes

Brotherly love. A little later he called back saying he kind of felt sorry for me and was on his way.

After we got back to camp, he pulled a few of those bigger thorns out of areas I couldn't reach. But he refused to touch my buttocks.

After driving the fourteen hours back to Iowa literally on pins and needles I realized my wife was still visiting a couple of our grandkids in Milwaukee. The first night at home in my own bed instead of the sleeping on the ground, cots and couches should have been great. But unfortunately, laying on my back the tiny broken off stubs of the hundreds of tiny thorns in my buttocks rubbed against the bed sheet constantly flicking those little nerve endings and waking me up. So... you have to picture this, I stuck long strips of that silver duct tape vertically all over my buttocks so the smooth silver side slid against the bed sheets. Perfect! Slept like a baby. A country boy will survive.

The next day I went to the clinic and got the bad news. I had a small break in the distal end of my right radius just above the wrist. No big problem other than I needed to immobilize it and couldn't shoot my bow for about six weeks.

Over a quarter of a century chasing hogs and I'd never been charged. Then I get charged twice in the same day. As I've said many times before, weird stuff always seems to happen to me. I should write a book or three... oh... never mind.

Always be aware any wounded animal might be dangerous. I'll never forget it the rest of my life. My only regret is it would have made for some great video footage... twice!

CHAPTER XXVII
THE MIDAS TOUCH

During the 2015 season I saw three of the four biggest bucks of that entire year from the same stand. Two of the three got downwind and boogered me. Then, in 2016 I tweaked the set-up but still didn't feel it was quite right. So, I moved the original stand about 60 yards. The stage was set.

The new stand position was the result of a combination of accumulated observations, new and old buck sign and reading the terrain.

Over the years I've laughed at guys who will be glued to a certain stand/position. They'll repeatedly see big buck movement, for example, sixty or seventy yards away, but out of range especially if they're bowhunting. They'll say to themselves, "man... there's something going on over there and someday I'm gonna figure it out!" What? What? Don't procrastinate, move your stand over there if at all possible. Maybe, you can figure out why they are moving better over there while you're in a better position to kill them. If you see a deer in a specific location once, it's an occurrence; if you see one in the same place twice you should perk up; if you see one there three times, you better move your buttocks or shame on you!

I always enjoy hunting a new stand for the first time. It's like starting a new chapter in a good book. So, it was on the afternoon of November 7, 2017. It was a beautiful fall day in the timber. Probably 55 degrees, sunny and maybe a 5 MPH breeze from the southwest.

I snuck into the new stand about 2PM that afternoon after a

wind switch forced me to leave another stand I'd been perched in all morning. This "felt" better. How could it get much better? This was Iowa, in a great, proven area, during the early stages of the whitetail rut. It was a fresh stand, never sat before, perfect wind and the fall foliage glowing yellow in the low afternoon sunlight. Life was good…. No, life was great!

When I first climbed into the ladder stand I set up my camcorder in hopes of maybe recording a kill. About 3:45 PM at about 80 yards to the south movement caught my eye. Walking west to east was a single, mature buck, all alone, out cruising for chicks. It was a strikingly pretty scene in the fall foliage colors and the low sunlight. I put my binoculars on him for a better look. He appeared to be a nice, mature buck in his prime. In all honesty, I really didn't intend to shoot him because I'd seen a potential B&C buck in the same general area both last year and the previous week. Sometimes my playful nature gets the best of me. It was early in the afternoon and I decided to mess with him just for grins and maybe get some good fall foliage, nice buck video footage.

As mentioned, he was about 80 yards away slowing walking in the dry leaves. I wheezed at him once and he never broke stride. A second wheeze still brought no reaction. I had a grunt tube with me so I gave it a blast. Nothing. I also had a rattle-bag hanging there so hit it and again, he never broke stride. I'm not sure if he was deaf or maybe the noise of him walking in the dry leaves overpowered my attempts to stir him up. Even so, I thought he definitely should have heard the rattling from 80 yards. But he just walked off and drifted away. As I said, I really wasn't very upset because I didn't intend to shoot him anyway.

About an hour later here he comes again. He was still walking west to east, which meant he must have made a big loop looking for the girls. I knew of two separate bedding areas not far away and suddenly it struck me that was what he was doing, sliding downwind of the two bedding areas scent checking the girls. But apparently all the beds were vacant. When he came by this time, he was only about fifty yards or so. I was just reaching for the camcorder when he suddenly turned and walked right towards me. The closer he got the better he looked. Even though he was pretty close I put the binoculars on him and decided he was a lot better than I first thought. His right antler was very unique, splitting into what looked like a palmated double main beam. Seriously, if his right antler had been" normal" and matched his left I would have let him walk. I'd already let a couple other bucks bigger than him walk earlier in October. I thought about the fact I hadn't shot a buck in the last two years; I'm getting old and I had two buck tags in my pocket. Yep... that right antler did him in.

Now, because of the angle he walked right towards me. I didn't dare reach for the camera. He was walking right down the major deer run that would pass me at 12 yards. When he got to fifteen yards, he did something that was rather strange by making a scrape right on the main run itself but out in the open with no overhanging limb or branches at all. I could have shot him right then but he was just very slightly quartering towards me. If I waited just a little while he would be perfectly broadside or quartering past me. The fact struck me this would have made great video footage. I again started to reach for the camcorder and here he came onwards... no time... sorry. He veered off the main run and frankly was too close at under ten yards. In order to not hit my lower bow limb on the side-rail of the ladder stand I had to reverse-cant my bow by tilting the top limb of my bow to my left, counter-clockwise. I almost instantly regretted it because it just didn't "feel right." The arrow almost hit a foot to the right of where I intended it to, but it blasted completely through him.

Sometimes things happen so quickly that your mind's-eye registers differently than reality. I think this was the case here as when I shot, I was confident he was perfectly broadside. But the arrow ripped right through his liver and angled out the paunch sticking in the ground.

He never had a clue what had just happened. He jumped forward two bounds and just stood there looking around. Even though he was still very close I could not get a finishing arrow into him because of the trees, branches, vines and brush. Still obscured by limbs, he stepped forward a couple more yards and bedded down. Within maybe five-minute intervals he stood up, took a few more steps and bedded back down three different times. I could tell he was really not doing well. A half hour later he was still bedded with his head up and appearing very alert. I was frustrated because I wanted to end it but I couldn't get an arrow through to him. And I knew if I climbed down and tried to advance on him, I'd likely run him out of the country.

Just before dark I heard a vehicle coming down the county road a few hundred yards away. This was a stroke of luck as normally a vehicle passes by only maybe once an hour. Another stroke of luck was it sounded like the vehicle needed the Midas Touch as he either had a giant hole in his muffler or no muffler at all. Using that stroke of luck to my advantage I made a quick decision. Leaving everything but my bow in the tree, I used the "No Midas Touch" background noise to bail out

The Midas Touch

He didn't make it fifty yards

and drop over the ridge crest to the north, then swung wide, downwind and out of sight praying at every step.

The next morning, I drove in with my four-wheeler rather than my truck, knowing I could get right to him (positive thinking). There he was. He hadn't made it fifty yards from point of impact. But I was alone. No one to take photos and the adapter I normally use to take self-portraits in the woods was in my truck. Yeah, I could have driven back to get the camera adapter but it was warm, mid-70s and I needed to get him out before he spoiled.

Long story short, I finally got him loaded up on the four-wheeler and home. But no "hero pictures", other than what I had to deal with. My apologies, I'll try better next time. Sorry. That's my story and I'm sticking to it.

CHAPTER XXVIII
SOUTHERN EXPOSURE

My brother Gene and I guided whitetail bowhunters along the Milk River of northeastern Montana for eight years back in the '90s. Since the total Montana deer season was eleven weeks in length, we would guide for two weeks, take a week off and guide for two more, etc. Gene and I would each take two bowhunters for seven weeks of the eleven-week season, for a total of 28 bowhunters per year. No brag… just fact, our bowhunters averaged right around 95% success rate for Pope and Young class bucks. Frankly, the only guys who didn't shoot a nice buck either were holding out for a monster or had missed. We were told the accumulated 200 plus record-book-class bucks was the highest success rate in the nation for free-ranging wild whitetails taken by bow and arrow at that time. It was a matter of quality managed lands and our knowledge of those lands and how to hunt them. It was excellent, rewarding and a lot of fun. But it also cut into a guy's personal hunting time.

Basically, left only with late season opportunities and normally severe Montana winters, there were still two months of great whitetail hunting opportunities available in our southern states. We, therefore, ended up hunting in Texas, Georgia, Alabama and Mississippi. For those of us northern whitetail fanatics who have not received our full dose of whitetail hunting, a post-season southern hunt should seriously be considered.

Some of the southern states have been given a bum rap when it comes to trophy hunting potential. Every one of the above-mentioned states has produced Boone and Crockett caliber bucks, especially so on managed properties. I personally would normally see bucks that would measure over 150 inches annually in the deep south. That's a nice buck anywhere you hunt whitetails.

Take Mississippi for example. In January of 1996 we hunted the Tara Wildlife Management area. It consisted of about 16,000 acres of prime bowhunting-only whitetail habitat. It was comprised of some of the best looking, lush river bottom habitat I've ever seen. With a multitude of high protein browse, coupled with no winter loss, a progressive management program and good basic genetics, it holds a bright future for whitetail hunters. There were lush green thickets of fertile terrain surrounded by agricultural crops and huge blocks of hardwood timber.

I'm very pleased to see various landowners turning their properties into bowhunting-only operations. Wise conservationists are now realizing bowhunters can effectively be used as a form of trophy management due to their limited range capabilities. For example, if you take a 5,000-acre managed area and turn ten "effective" rifle hunters onto it for a week, they'd most likely shoot ten good bucks. But if you take that same 5,000-acre area and instead, turn twenty of the world's best bowhunters loose on it for a week, they'd certainly get a few good bucks, but they won't be as detrimental to the age structure of the herd simply because of the range limitations of their weapons.

I really enjoy the diversity of the terrain in the Deep South. You sometimes can have your choice of either hunting the palmetto swamps, planted pines or vast hardwoods. The third day of my '96 hunt saw me positioned in a 22-foot high treestand overlooking a hardwood flat. That beautiful afternoon

I saw twenty-five deer, including three nice racked bucks. The bucks were rutting, chasing does all over the place. It was great.

Even though the terrain appeared flat I could detect some structural diversity. Subtle variations such as minor land contours due to previous river floodwaters, as well as deviations in the overhead canopy will result in changes in light intensities, which, in turn, alter secondary vegetative growth. Additionally, some fallen timber, either from a storm or maybe spring flooding, had created minor travel pattern changes.

Does appeared to be using a fifty-yard-wide strip of button willows in their normal travel pattern. I decided to sacrifice about a half hour of mid-day hunting time to quickly scout the area. It paid off. About eighty yards from my treestand I found a double sycamore that covered three major runs. And more importantly, there was a line of eight fresh scrapes going past it. The strip of willows ran northeast/ southwest. The winds had been coming out of the south or southwest for the last couple of days.

The local weather forecast predicted a switch to a northerly wind for the next couple of days. Even though I'm a huge fan of weighing and playing the odds, the newly predicted wind direction would be real borderline. In all honesty I like a wind that is "almost wrong". I always have. It tends to give a buck a false sense of security if you can depend on directional consistency. In other words, on a southwest to northeast movement with the wind out of the north, the buck would feel some false security in an "almost" headwind, especially in fairly open hardwoods where he can see.

I repositioned the stand mid-morning the next day. That afternoon I decided to hunt a different area in order to give any residual ground scent enough time to dissipate.

The following morning, I entered the stand via pre-set cat-eye reflector tacks. I wasn't in the new set-up for fifteen minutes when a slight noise alerted me. Here he came... right down the scrape line... just like he was "supposed" to. He hit the first three scrapes doing the overhead branch thing. I was going to take him when he angled past to the fourth. About halfway between the third and fourth, he suddenly locked up broadside at fourteen yards. I'm not sure if he got a whiff of ground-scent or what, but he immediately went on red-alert. Unfortunately for him it was too late as I was already almost at full draw. I locked in and visually bored a hole through his ribs. Letting the string quietly slip from my fingers he instinctively tried to wheel but the broadhead split his heart. The shaft broke off on his far side as he raced off. I watched him crash through the willows for sixty yards before his lights went out and he went down.

He was a nice 4x4 with decent mass and a broken tine on one side that I didn't even notice before I shot. I ended up getting a four-wheeler right up to him. My kind of drag! He later weighted in at 198 pounds but was aged at only 2 ½ years old. That absolutely blew me away because looking at his body size and characteristics, I honestly thought he was older. I mean, this is the Deep South and I wasn't expecting many bucks kissing 200 lbs., no less when they are only 2 ½. I was obviously fooled by the quality of the local younger bucks, another tribute to quality deer management.

Even though my season had just come to an end, I still found myself wishing for more time. Just one more week! Then it hit me, I'd been guiding or bowhunting whitetails almost every day since September 1st.

My kind of drag!

Three solid months in Montana, then a full week in Texas; another week in Georgia; another week in Alabama and still another week in Mississippi... and here I was wishing for just one more week. I admit it... that my friends... is not normal.

Sometimes one does not need to wait until late winter to

enjoy the rewards of southern hospitality. I believe it was mid-October of 1992 when I had the opportunity to sandwich and Alabama bow hunt into one of our "off" weeks between guiding Montana hunters. Due to some interesting circumstances, I was offered a chance to bow hunt a private 4,000-acre hunting club along the Alabama River south of Selma.

After arriving and touring the property, I asked the club manager to take me to the thickest, most remote cover he knew of on the place. I was impressed to say the least. Usually, it takes several days to find "that spot" where all the pieces of the whitetail puzzle come together. In fact, all too often it's the last day of the season, or the last day of a hunt before I find "the" spot. But then again, if you're like me, these last-minute discoveries whet our appetite to give us something to dream about until next year. Of course, when you return a year later, we find conditions have changed and we're forced to sometimes start all over again. That's one of the reasons relentless scouting pays off.

One of my good friends, Wayne Fisher from Florida and I were shown an old roadway cutting through mixed hardwoods and pines, near the remains of a turn of the century homestead. Because of the abandoned homestead the canopy was open and the ground vegetation was thick beyond belief with lush vegetation, vines and honeysuckle. I instinctively knew this was where the big boys lived. It was the kind of spot I'd been hoping for.

Wayne, by the way, is recognized as one of the top cobia/marlin fishermen on the Florida Gulf coast. He's also one of the most knowledgeable southern whitetail fanatics I've ever met.

After an hour or so of intense scouting, Wayne and I hung a stand for myself along a hardwood ridge with a saddle containing half a dozen fresh rubs on trees with diameters of five to six inches. We also located three, smoking fresh, new scrapes. Remember, this was mid-October in the Deep South where daytime temps often hang in the 90s with humidity. This sign was textbook perfect.

Sign indicated a good buck was coming through the hardwoods and saddle, skirting the edge of a weed field, cutting across a hardwood swale and entering thick pines to bed. We backed off to let the area settle down.

Generally, one doesn't think of Alabama as a top trophy region, however, the area's nutritional quality, combined with an effective deer management program give this Black Belt region the potential to produce Boone and Crockett class bucks each year. Based on what I saw there was no doubt in my mind a true monster could be taken here in time.

I wanted to make my first hunt in the area an afternoon/evening so I could cat-eye my way in while it was still dark. Plus, I wanted to clip away some vines and thick understory to quiet my approach the next day. The following afternoon I entered a little early and cut my way into my stand. Other than a coon, two armadillos, a 'possum, dozens of squirrels, a flock of turkeys and three does, I didn't see much. Then, just as the sun slid behind the treetops at my back, I caught the shine of antlers. He was probably a hundred yards away. All I got was a glimpse because of the heavy vegetation but I could see he had a good rack. I patiently waited until full dark before quietly sneaking out.

Before pink light the next morning I parked my truck farther away to create as little disturbance as possible to the area. When I hit the edge of the pine thicket and weed field, rather than taking the most logical approach along the old roadway, I took advantage of my knee-high rubber boots and flashlight where I'd cut around the edge and up through the hardwood swale I'd cleared the day before. That way, any approaching buck would be least likely to cut my entering track.

About twenty minutes after first shooting light my eye caught movement. Already standing I reached over to unhook my recurve hanging from a nearby branch. The buck was about forty yards out, skirting the edge of the weed field. As he hit the first scrape, he only hesitated a second or two before continuing on to the next scrape. He paused a little longer here sniffing the overhead limb but he never worked the ground. It was obvious he was just going through the motions of pre-rut activity. I got the impression the scrapes were there because they were in his normal movement pattern; he wasn't there because of the scrapes... if that makes sense.

His lack of real interest was obvious when he just glanced at the third scrape and never actually approached it. But his direction of travel to the bedding area took him through a good shooting lane at about 20 yards. I was tempted but waited when I noticed a clear lane that would offer a better shooting angle at fifteen yards. Timing his pace, I drew down and let the string slip from my fingers as his shoulder passed through the second opening. My broadhead went in one side and out the other cutting off the top of his heart. He turned and ran back towards the way he'd entered, crashing hard about seventy-five yards away where the old skid road cut along the edge of the weed field.

A fine tribute to southern deer potential

After watching his still form for a few seconds, I climbed down from my perch and retrieved what was left of my arrow, replacing it in my quiver. Tracking wasn't really necessary but I walked along the ample blood trail to where he laid. This was my kind of deer. I was forced to drag him maybe ten or twelve feet to where he could be loaded in the back of my truck from the tote road.

A beautiful representative of a southern whitetail, he had a short-haired coat that revealed muscle tone more readily than northern deer at this time of year. Being it was mid-October he had his winter coat but it wasn't as think as the northern coats were.

Although his rack wouldn't score well because of asymmetry, it showed a lot of character. The left side had four points with the bez tine measuring eleven inches and a long, curving brow tine that had a windswept look. The right antler only sported three points but the right main beam swept up to perfectly match the left trez, giving the rack a very uniform appearance even though asymmetrical.

Examination of his teeth revealed he was only three and a half years old. These southern bucks will fool you. I thought he was going to be at least five and a half. Had his right antler matched his left he would have measured 144 inches... but I wasn't complaining. Weighing in at 210 pounds back at camp, he was a great buck considering we were within a hundred miles of Florida. I also later found out he was the best buck that had ever been taken from that club property at that time with either gun or bow, a fine tribute to southern deer potential and proper land/deer management.

CHAPTER XXIX
THE HUNDRED-YEAR-OLD MAN

On the morning of November 19, 2012, I had a really interesting, thought provoking, experience. I've been a whitetail fanatic for over sixty years. That morning I passed up an old veteran buck which I believe was the oldest whitetail I've ever seen. I obviously have no way to prove it but he looked absolutely ancient. The big non-typical buck I shot in 2011 was judged to be 9.5 years old. This buck could have been his grand daddy. His antlers had degenerated to next to nothing, I'm certain barely a shadow of his prime years. They were basically massive spikes with a bunch of heavy beading, no main beam but a slightly bladed tiny fork at the top of his one antler.

All alone, I watched him come to me from a hundred yards through the open hardwoods. He was a "slow walker", but not because he was waiting for thermal currents to change. He was obviously in pain... like a very old man with high mileage. It took him a solid fifteen minutes to walk a hundred yards. I thought about doing a mercy-killing because he looked in such poor shape. I took some video footage of him at fifteen yards. Sadly, I could see the age/pain in his face and eyes. He looked gaunt and was having a hard time simply walking on level ground. I knew he had arthritic hips and a kyphotic (humped) spine. I knew he wouldn't make the upcoming winter but I had to respect his unwavering tenacity.

I wondered what he looked like when he was in his prime; how much he weighed; how big his rack was; how many trophy bucks he sired and outlived; how many times he survived sub-zero temperatures with winds howling at 25 MPH while he

A truly ancient deer

hunkered down under a pine as his only protection on a basically empty stomach; how many red-coats he'd made it by; the gangbangers, the in-line muzzleloader guys with their "primitive" weapons with thumb-hole stocks, bi-pods and scopes who can shoot them in the head from hundreds of yards? Not to mention the late-season antlerless rifle shooters who pop the biggest antlerless deer from 200 yards only to find out it's a shed mature buck. Then, there are the packs of deer running dogs, coyotes, bobcats, increased vehicular traffic and the local rednecks who just closed the local bar and shouldn't even be driving but are headed home with a spotlight out the window.

Harsh conditions, drought, severe heat/humidity while wearing a fur coat, floods, fires, ticks, chiggers, horse flies, wasps and bees, he was a true survivor. I also guarantee he watched me in the woods many more times than I watched him over the years. I had plenty of time to think about the situation.

In the 2006 season I was after a beautiful buck I'd nicknamed "Rocky." In fact, I wrote a chapter about my pursuit of him, complete with photos in my book, "Once Upon A Tine" after having eleven (yes... eleven) encounters including four very close calls that season. I later found out one of the neighbor's relatives ultimately killed Rocky during the late gun season. Rumor had it he ended up measuring in the low 170s as a four-year-old when I thought he was five.

Because I only had a single buck tag in 2006 and had my heart set on Rocky, I passed up several outstanding trophies that year. One I recalled was very special. It was hard for me not to kill him but my constant close calls with Rocky kept me on track. This buck was a basic 4x4 but he had extreme mass at the bases and a conglomeration of multiple extra points protruding between his brow tines and pedicles. It appeared he had a whole cluster of extra points around his bases. I remember thinking about the potential damage an aggressive rack like that could do to a stout rubbing tree. I estimated him as likely 5.5 years old and in his prime. In fact, I took some video footage of him one afternoon as he walked by me at 18 yards. If it hadn't been for Rocky and myself only having one buck tag, I would have killed this one in a heartbeat. He was a heavyweight contender as well, very likely to dress out at over 250 solid pounds. I actually passed him up twice in 2006 while I hunted

I had my heart set on Rocky

Rocky, both times as he followed a doe with obvious intentions.

Later that winter while visiting with a local landowner, he brought up the subject of that particular buck. Because of his unique antler configurations, I knew we were talking about the same buck. He informed me they almost got him in an organized drive but he got away... but "we ran him out of the country." I didn't see the stud the following two years in his old turf. I figured maybe one of the fragments of flying lead might have unknowingly found its mark after all. Or, like so many other specific, recognizable bucks we watch, he just melted away.

Around 2009 we started seeing another "similar" buck in a big block of timber almost a mile north of where I hunted Rocky. I probably should have recognized him but enough years had passed, the land had been bought and sold and I no longer had permission to hunt it. Frankly, I forgot about the 2006 buck. I don't think this "new" buck just showed up as much as the fact we started hunting more frequently where he lived. We even nick-named the new heavyweight "Knarly." His body size was enormous. I had several close encounters with Knarly in both 2009 and 2010 but I only had one tag left and I was now in hot pursuit of Hurley. I remember thinking if Knarly and Hurley ever went head-to-head, mono-a-mono it would be a great heavyweight division match-up. Although Hurley's rack might have been a little bigger, Knarly had the bigger body (and Hurley later field-dressed 248 lbs.). Knarly also had more mass in his beams. In fact, I feared there would absolutely be broken tines skipping through the leaves.

Then, all of a sudden it struck me, could this ancient buck I was now looking at possibly be the same buck I passed in 2006? Could multiple close calls with the gun hunting and organized deer drives on the adjoining farm actually "run him out of the country?" Would he give up his original home turf for beautiful timber less than a mile away that was only bowhunted by a couple fat guys... who he knew already let him walk in the past? If my original estimate was correct and he was in fact 5.5 years old in 2006, that would calculate that I was looking at a potential 11.5-year-old true survivor.

As I watched the old man walk, I felt genuinely sorry for him. I've had to put good dogs down in the past. I absolutely hated it and even cried. I thought about justifying the kill, but the meat would likely not even be palatable. I have a personal thing about old animals. I have absolutely no desire to shoot an elephant because he might be older than I am. I have no problem with someone else doing it, that's just me. I continue to have a soft spot in my heart for old things. Age usually means

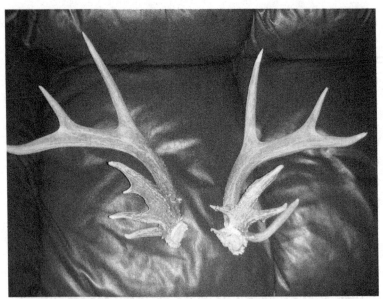

I believe these are some sheds of a younger 100-year-old man

wisdom and wisdom usually demands respect. Yes, I managed the hunting on the farm he lived on. We gave him the chance to grow old by keeping it limited to bowhunting only. I was torn. I understand we are to be stewards of the land and the game. Maybe I'm getting soft in my older years. Even though I had an extra tag in my pocket in 2012, I felt sorry for him. Maybe I got too good of a look at his face and in his eyes.

I ultimately decided to let him walk, to live out the rest of his life as nature intended. As I watched him slowly walk away, I honestly got choked up. I prayed his last year didn't end in a violent death. I hoped he died in his sleep. I'm still not sure if I made the right decision.

As unbelievable as this may be, on October 1, 2013, the opening morning of the 2013 Iowa bow season, I was sitting in a stand in a giant, double oak a half mile from the stand mentioned above. I normally have no intention of shooting a buck this early in the season but I always go for tradition.

I remember the sky was clear and the morning sun was already up, so any passing deer were running late. Movement caught my eye. I absolutely couldn't believe it, there he was! The now 101-year-old man was slowly limping his way up to his bedroom. How could he possibly survive the past brutal winter, in an area infested with coyotes? I would have assumed any coyote that laid eyes on him would instantly see him as an easy meal. No way... but it was absolutely him. I recognized his face and eyes when I put the binoculars on him.

I never lifted my new bow from the hanging bow-hook. As he walked past at twenty yards, I stood up out of respect, like I do for our American flag. My movement caught his attention verifying he wasn't blind. He stopped and turned his head looking right at me. As corny as it sounds, I saluted him as he walked away, never to be seen again.

I'll tell you one thing is for sure, God did good when He made bucks like that and granted us the opportunity to pursue them. Thank you Lord!

ABOUT THE AUTHOR

Barry Wensel has been sharing his whitetail wisdom for well over fifty years. He's written close to a hundred published magazine articles; authored, co-authored or been featured in a dozen hunting books. He's additionally appeared in a multitude of national outdoor TV shows; produced and/or been featured in a couple dozen hunting videos since the early 1980s. He's been a popular seminar speaker at literally all the various state Whitetail Deer Classics and major sport shows nationally for close to forty years. He ran the first three-day, all-inclusive "whitetail school/ bootcamps," teaching his unique whitetail hunting strategies, while handing down his hunting techniques to sold out crowds for a total of fifteen years. Additionally, in one seven-year stint, he and his brother, Gene, guided whitetail bowhunters to over 200 record-book class, free-ranging whitetail bucks. Yes, his uncommon techniques work very well.

Barry and his loving wife of 56 years, Susan, are the proud parents of three grown children and five grandchildren scattered from Wisconsin to Montana and all the way to Australia. Barry and Susan presently reside in the farmlands of rural Iowa.

For additional copies of this book, to book Whitetail seminars and/or hunting DVD's and videos please contact:

Barry Wensel Productions
P.O. Box 155
Lineville, IA 50147
barrywensel@hotmail.com

Made in the USA
Middletown, DE
13 February 2025